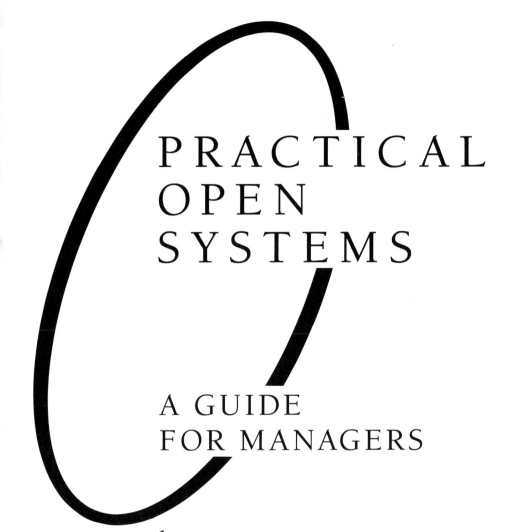

PRACTICAL OPEN SYSTEMS

A GUIDE FOR MANAGERS

by

IAN HUGO

Data General

NCC Blackwell

MANCHESTER • OXFORD

British Library Cataloguing in Publication Data
A guide to practical open systems.
  1. Computer systems
  I. Data General Ltd
  004

  ISBN 1-85554-079-7

First published in 1991 by:

NCC Blackwell Limited, 108 Cowley Road, Oxford OX4 1JF,
England.

Editorial Office: The National Computing Centre Limited, Oxford
House, Oxford Road, Manchester M1 7ED, England.

Typeset in 11pt Palatino by Bookworm Typesetting, Manchester;
and printed by Hobbs the Printers of Southampton.

ISBN 1-85554-079-7

Dedication

**To Natalie and Carl,
my muses**

Acknowledgements

Thanks go to the staff at Data General for the assistance they provided in the writing of this book.

Trademark acknowledgements are due to the following companies:

Digital Equipment
  DECNET
  PDP
  ULTRIX
  VAX
  VMS

International Business Machines Corporation
  AD/Cycle
  AIX
  Micro Channel
  MVS
  OS/2
  Presentation Manager
  PS/2
  Repository Manager/MVS
  SAA

Microsoft Corporation
  LAN Manager
  MS-DOS
  Xenix

Novell
  Netware

Sun Microsystems
  NFS

Unix Systems Laboratories Inc
  Open Look
  UNIX

Contents

1   Introduction

READ ME (PLEASE)

This book is intended as a guide to practical open systems for IT managers. It provides explanations of the major concepts involved and contains lists of sources of more detailed information. It is not intended to be the "compleat" work on the subject, but a handy reference book—a primary source. Above all, it is aimed at increasing understanding of the mechanisms at play in the emerging field of practical open systems. What is important now is that IT managers should understand the major shift in direction that the IT industry is currently undergoing and, broadly, how and why. The book is therefore aimed more at strategic thinking than at immediate problem solving, bearing in mind that now may actually be the time to start changing strategy.

The term "practical" is used to denote a wider context than just those systems that conform to the standards agreed by the international standards organisations. We also include a consideration of the standards set by significant alliances of suppliers and of important de facto proprietary standards. The reason for extending the scope of open systems beyond its most common bounds is, quite simply, pragmatism.

Formal international standards, as they are sometimes called, are currently inadequate for the full implementation of many applications (although progress is constantly being made). Also, there are very few "green field" installations that can start with a clean sheet; the very large majority have a considerable investment in proprietary architectures, and any move towards open systems must take account of these.

A policy of moving to open systems cannot mean that all new

systems must conform to formal international standards. Neither can development be delayed until all necessary standards are formally defined. In the interim, de facto and alliance standards provide many of the benefits of "pure" open systems, and are a move in the right direction. Initially, the only feasible objective in some cases will be to seek "more open" rather than "pure open" systems, making gains in interoperability at the very least.

For these practical reasons, the assumption is that a policy of open systems will embrace formal standards where they meet the need and, as a positioning move in this direction, will seek de facto or alliance standards in preference to narrow proprietary environments where they do not meet the need.

The term "IT managers" is intended to refer to any staff working in IT with a managerial (rather than a technically specialised) role or perspective. This book does contain some quite technical material, suitably explained, where there are technical considerations that managers should understand. However, it is unlikely to satisfy the technician's typical thirst for technical detail and is not intended to do so.

The book attempts to cover the main arguments applicable to practical open systems, and explains most of the relevant concepts, with frequent use of analogies. It also seeks to provide a first level of sources of further information and of other forms of help. No extensive directories are included as this would simply duplicate existing publications; directories and lists of various sorts can be obtained from the first-level sources given in this book.

Above all, the book seeks to explain the new framework for practical open systems and to provide a primary source of understanding and reference for IT managers who seek the advantages that an open systems policy can provide.

THE BROAD PICTURE

Here comes the first analogy. It is important to understand the context for open systems because of the very significant implications that they have for the whole structure of the IT industry. What is going on is analogous to redrawing the political map of the world and at the same time discovering a better way of describing its physical geography.

Describing the political map of the world, in its current state of flux, requires some caution. However, it has been fashionable to think broadly in terms of two power blocs, designated east and west, and a large number of much smaller, individual, non-aligned countries. In fact, interwoven with this general structure are further groupings of countries on the basis of geography (eg the EEC) or of special interests (eg OPEC).

To the extent that the political map can be said to be a representation of the way in which particular peoples have colonised the physical globe and grouped themselves, so a "political" map of IT would be a representation of the way in which computer suppliers have "colonised" the user community. The divisions between groupings in this case, however, are not national frontiers but proprietary machine environments. As in the political world, there are various other groupings within the IT world, both with regard to geography (eg national standards organisations) and with regard to special interests (eg OSF, UI). In fact, the general shape of the world political map looks rather similar to the general shape of the IT "political" map, with similar kinds of forces for change at work.

You may, if you wish, have some fun pursuing this analogy. However, one important point of the analogy is that, just as the world political map is changing, so too is the IT "political map". Proprietary "frontiers" are coming down; many suppliers are surrendering some "sovereignty" in favour of larger alliances, much as is happening within the EEC; and the whole direction of IT "politics" is being driven more and more by the community of users under the slow but remorseless blessing of an IT "United Nations"—the International Standards Organisation (in fact, a UN agency).

So much for the changing political map; the IT equivalent to the physical globe is a logical map of IT. Unlike the usual physical geography, the logical geography of IT has never been properly described; there has never been an accepted paradigm for IT that would allow such a description to be made. In the absence of a general paradigm, the world is described from the bottom up, rather than from the top down; more general structures have to be devised empirically, through experience. That is still the case, but we are now discovering some better general structures, as evidenced by object orientation, client-server architectures, OSI, SAA, PCTE, etc.

The lack of general structures has often been the cause in the past of specific tools and techniques that were heralded as great productivity aids which failed to deliver on the promises. Tools have generally been conceived to address very specific problems, in the absence of a wider framework that could specify where their interfaces to other problem areas should be. Each tool maps the logical geography of IT differently and locates natural frontiers in different places. Because of this, the sub-optimisations that they offer conflict with the other tools that have been similarly designed to address other specific questions. The tools fail to deliver fully because of conflicts that can be resolved only by a standard description of the wider context within which they should work.

This problem has been addressed by some suppliers when defining proprietary architectures, such as SAA, SNA, AIA, etc. More significantly, it is being addressed by alliances of suppliers, and by national and international standards organisations. The important point to understand is that the beginning of any solution to this problem is a generally agreed mapping of the logical geography of areas of IT—in effect, a reference model (see *Important aspects of standards* in Chapter 5). The reference model effectively describes a logical area and the geography within it—where particular functions are located and where their interfaces to other functions should be.

That work is now quite advanced and is proceeding at an increasing rate. It is at the very heart of the promise of open systems and is more important than the consideration of who "owns" the model. Ideally, it should be owned by an international standards organisation, but such bodies move relatively slowly. Individual suppliers have the resources to design a reference model and populate it with products, so they may move fastest, but this may also lead to problems of "locking in" and increased costs. Alliances of suppliers in significant numbers, if stable, provide many of the benefits and few of the drawbacks.

This book assumes that users will wish to operate within these types of environment in preference to using ad hoc individual systems that are locked into a single supplier. In the past, users have had little alternative, but they now have increasing opportunities for moving to a much less restrictive and potentially much more cost-effective basis for IT. We have attempted to show how and why this is.

2 What are open systems?

DIFFICULTIES IN DEFINITION

Not long ago, at a press conference called by the UK Government to announce an initiative on open systems, the minister and assembled senior civil servants were asked to define "open systems". They all declined. The refusal was disconcerting but understandable. The term is difficult to define and means many different things to different people.

It is not often that a government decides to spend £12 million on something it can't or won't define. What was certain, given a government that was not in favour of subsidies, was that open systems must be considered important.

That still leaves the problem of definition. A handbook on open systems needs a definition, and a good definition must convey not just the literal sense but also the real meaning of a term. So what we will do is work up to a definition through an understanding of why the term was coined. We'll begin with a very little history.

IN THE BEGINNING

The very first computers were programmed either in a form of binary code or in a very primitive assembly language that was quite specific to the machine involved. The same job on another machine, even one from the same supplier, would need to be totally reprogrammed. Computer users were essentially "locked into" their current machine; if they changed machine, they would have to rewrite all their programs.

That situation changed in the mid-1960s, when IBM announced

the 360 Series. The idea was that there should be a series of essentially similar machines, all of which ran under one operating system — OS/360. Users could thus start with a relatively small computer, and as the number of jobs increased, and with it the volume of work to be processed on the computer, so they could move to a larger machine without having to reprogram everything. Users would no longer be locked into a specific machine (although they would still be locked into a specific operating system).

The reality, of course, differed somewhat from the theory. It proved to be a lot more difficult than had initially been thought to shield programs from differences between even similar machines; and, anyway, other factors intruded between the users and their promised land.

It was true that users could move between machines in the same series (from the same supplier) with much less difficulty. But it was also true that they were still locked into the particular series of machines (and supplier) that they were using currently. Moreover, that is generally still the case today.

Most other machine suppliers of the time, and all that have since come into the market, adopted the idea of an essentially similar (compatible) series of machines and a single operating system (albeit in multiple versions) under which they ran. Nowadays, a series (or range) of machines and the operating system they work under is generally called an "operating environment" and reference is made to "proprietary" and "open" environments.

"Open" environments have their origins in the standards organisations that have worked to create uniformity among suppliers. As with all bodies whose goal is to extract agreements from companies and nations with differing interests, the procedures often seem laborious and progress slow. Nonetheless, there has been progress, resulting in the definition of major portions of an overall operating environment.

"Proprietary" environments belong to a single supplier, as the term suggests, and are the prevailing case for most users currently. Open environments are currently the minority case but are still developing. These are where the future lies and are what this handbook is about.

ELEMENTS OF OPEN SYSTEMS

As we indicated at the beginning, open systems mean many different things to different people. Some think immediately of Open Systems Interconnection (OSI)—a developing definition of a standard means of networking computers that is being agreed by the International Standards Organisation. That is certainly an important part of the picture, but not all of it.

Some people think immediately of the UNIX operating system— an operating system created originally around 1970 by Ken Thompson of Bell Laboratories, in order to run his workstation the way he wanted it to work. UNIX subsequently found favour in the academic and research community quite generally, with the result that thousands of graduates wanted to use it in their subsequent commercial work. From there, it has been picked up by most major computer suppliers and has become the subject of international standardisation efforts. UNIX too is an important part of the picture, but not all of it.

Some people are less concerned with networking and operating systems than with developing applications. They think of an open software development environment and of the work being done by standards bodies to create a definition for an Information Resource Dictionary System (IRDS). That too is another part of the picture.

Finally, in a definition of truly open systems, it would be wrong to discount totally all proprietary systems. That may seem a contradiction and so needs a little explanation.

There are some proprietary environments that have gained a very large market share and are not totally within the grasp of the supplier. Let us give two examples.

The more tenuous, but more arguable, of the two is the IBM 370 architecture market. There is no doubt that IBM controls the general environment, in terms of the major operating system and subsystem software. However, users who have this environment have some choice in terms of PCM hardware and competitive third-party software. There is no doubt that MVS and VM/VSE is currently the dominant environment for large data centres.

The second, more obvious, example is that of MS-DOS/PC-DOS.

In the case of MS-DOS, it is quite clear that Microsoft, who produced it, does not in any sense control the huge market of applications and machines created to run under that environment. Again, it is a dominant environment and, technically at least, it is a proprietary environment.

In such cases, truly open systems should provide a means of linking to these environments. Investment in them is such that it will continue for some time to come. If that impacts the "purity" of our definition, so be it. The objective is not to be holier but above all to be more open, since it is through openness that users ultimately gain. Any dominant proprietary environment, at any given time, will need to be recognised by an open-systems supplier.

All these elements, and others besides, help to build our definition of open systems. We are getting close, but there is one side of the picture that we need to look at before we attempt a definition ourselves. What should users hope to gain from deciding to opt for open systems? This subject also is dealt with in detail in a separate section, but we will look briefly at some of the major motivations here.

POSSIBLE GAINS AND ACTUAL LOSSES

In western economies, it is generally accepted that the greatest progress can be made by the free competition of ideas and developments within a guiding framework of law. Applied to computers, this means that suppliers should be encouraged to compete to produce the best technology and the most suitable services, in order to attract the most clients. The computing industry should be no different from any other in this respect.

However, as we have already noted, the large majority of users is currently locked into proprietary environments. This means, in practice, that although a supplier may, at any one time, produce a product or service that is clearly superior to that of the competition, the cost of converting to a new supplier may negate any possible gain.

Since the cost of conversion between proprietary environments is generally high, and gets higher as the user's investment in computing grows, the only gains that are feasible to contemplate are, effectively, quantum leaps. Very few areas of human endeavour progress only by quantum leaps; significant progress is more normally the result of a succession of small steps in the right direction. Open systems hold the promise to allow that; proprietary systems cannot.

To defend proprietary environments, we have to assume that the supplier who "owns" that environment not only has the best product/service for all tasks currently but will always have the best answer. To be able to take advantage of the strengths of different suppliers for different tasks at different points in time, users must be able to choose between suppliers without encountering any major cost barriers imposed by their existing investment.

That is the major gain promised by open systems and the major challenge to be met.

AT LAST—A DEFINITION

We now have the elements necessary to create our definition of open systems and, it is hoped, a reasonable background understanding of the underlying issues. The principal elements of the definition are:

— the freedom to choose between suppliers' offerings without a significant conversion penalty;

— the means of accommodating all aspects of producing and running applications:

- software development,
- production running,
- networking;

— the work of standards organisations;

— the acknowledgement of dominant, existing, proprietary environments.

It must also be acknowledged that work still remains to be done before truly open systems are achieved, and that there are technical as well as political difficulties involved.

So for the purposes of this handbook the following is our definition:

"Open systems are those that conform to internationally agreed standards defining computing environments
that allow users to develop, run and interconnect
applications and the hardware they run on, from
whatever source, without significant conversion cost."

The really key factors for the users are that no single supplier
actually "owns" the environments involved, and that the mixing
and matching of applications and hardware can be achieved
without significant cost. We could quibble at what "significant"
means, but there must clearly be some cost in changing
applications or equipment. The point here is that users should not
be denied better products or services because of incompatibility
between proprietary environments, and that internationally
agreed standards, where they exist, should be used.

3 Why change to open systems?

THE PRINCIPLE

In principle, it is easy to accept that an open market, in which the major elements of computer systems are commodities to be bought and assembled, much in the same way as one buys and uses consumer goods, must be to the advantage of users. The only obvious question is why that is not the case already.

Some explanation for the current domination of proprietary environments has already been given. This section explains the major changes in economics and technology that are causing the shift to open systems, turning what has been a pipe-dream into reality.

THE ROLE OF INVESTMENT

Users

Over time, all users have seen their investment in IT grow. Despite occasional cutbacks, false starts, restarts and some well-publicised disasters, the march of IT investment over time has been inexorable. It is sometimes said that the principal part of this investment is in staff skills and data rather than machinery and programs. Be that as it may, it is all more or less locked into proprietary environments; and the greater the investment, the more the user is locked in.

Moreover, the nature and number of applications today is such that few businesses of any size could operate without computer systems. It is no longer feasible to contemplate doing away with computers or simply throwing out one version of a major application from one supplier in favour of another proprietary solution.

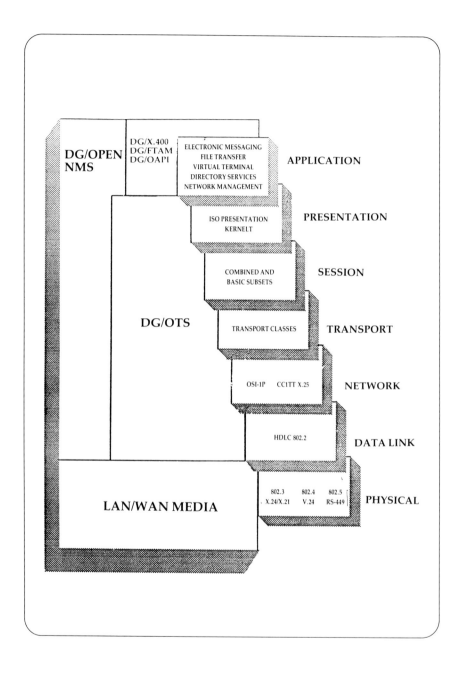

Figure 3.1   DG/OSI Communications Architecture Solutions

Modern management thinking, however, proposes a flexible role for IT, suggesting a major role for it as a marketing tool, exploiting opportunities for new services aimed at gaining competitive edge. That stance conflicts directly with the dead weight of investment in proprietary systems. With the best will in the world, IT departments cannot introduce new business solutions from an arbitrary variety of different vendors and hope to survive. They must look to their major supplier for nearly all their requirements.

This conflict has produced a focus on "architectures" in the large corporate organisations (*see* Figure 3.1 sample architectural solutions). What this means, in effect, is a directive to IT departments to select a proprietary environment that is broad enough in scope and rich enough in function to encompass all foreseen needs, and only to buy systems that operate within that environment.

This is a tenable approach, and indeed the only feasible one if we assume that proprietary environments will dominate forever. However, its efficacy depends on the assumption that at least some suppliers, together with their third-party markets, can provide the breadth and depth of solutions required. As the scope of IT has progressed, fewer have been able to fill the bill, resulting in frustration for users and an increasing tendency to operate under de facto proprietary "standards". That is not a satisfactory solution, and western governments in particular have been active in promoting the open alternative.

Suppliers

As has been noted above, any vendor who wishes to supply large corporations is forced by the expansion of IT to offer an ever wider range of products and services. This implies either a constantly increasing percentage of revenues devoted to R&D and/or an increasingly thinner spread of those resources across the board. In practice, most vendors have been forced to withdraw from the general market and focus on niches.

This tendency has recently extended to the third-party software markets. Any new entrant to the third-party market naturally looks at the size of proprietary "ponds" available to swim in. As the number of generally viable suppliers dwindles, so does the feasible choice for third-party vendors, forcing the third-party market into fewer "ponds". This in turn makes the lagging proprietary environments less viable, generating a continuous spiral that tends to force all resources into one or two proprietary environments.

For existing third-party suppliers, a natural defence against new entrants is to grow larger and faster, thus effectively increasing the price of entry into the market. The normal way to grow larger quickly is by acquisition, and that is what has been happening. However, extensive competing product lines create the same drawback for third-party suppliers as for the owners of the proprietary environments; they cannot afford to develop and support all the products, so some have to be dropped.

The net effect of all these factors is that innovation and price performance suffer. In the past it has been the smaller new entrants to the market-place that have been noted for innova-tion—the very companies who will increasingly become less able to afford the entry price. This is also the type of company that has frequently broken new ground in price performance, as other breakthroughs result from competition for market share between several vendors. For how much longer can many large vendors, and many small third-party suppliers, exist in a market-place dominated by one or two proprietary environments?

Open systems

It is obvious that open systems provide a solution to the problems described. Essentially, open systems allow all investment to flow into the same "pond", allowing innovation to proceed faster and demolishing entry-price barriers. However, the fact that the solution is there is not enough to make it actually happen.

What has made it happen, and will continue to do so, is the fact that most vendors will tolerate the spiral no longer. All vendors have now acknowledged a role for open systems, and all but the very largest have declared that their major future product development will be in the open-systems arena. An important factor here is that the aggregated market bases of all the smaller vendors create a "pond" that is larger than the largest proprietary environments. That fact, and the aggregated R&D budgets of the smaller vendors, ensure that open systems will be the environ-ment of the future. And the future starts now.

CONTRIBUTORY CRISES

The spiral described above, which leads to a concentration on a few proprietary environments, shows its limitations in the way that it exacerbates many of the difficulties that have faced (or are now facing) the IT industry.

One example comes from IBM's announcement of its Systems Application Architecture (SAA). IBM is by far the largest player in the computer industry; it understood and responded to the market need for an architecture to provide a framework for all system development. The IBM architecture is sound and is based on IBM proprietary environments, yet IBM chose to herald the architecture as "open". Why?

The simple fact is that even IBM cannot single-handedly fund all the research and development necessary to produce the full range of products required for the satisfactory implemention of the architecture. IBM has therefore forged some alliances, left some parts of the architecture open to all comers, and strategically retained some for itself. Faced with a research problem it cannot fund itself, this is a reasonable position for the owner of a proprietary environment to take.

However, that is only one aspect, albeit a major one, of IT. The control of operations, data centres and networks are others. These are market requirements, and if IBM alone cannot fund them, who alone can? The answer has to lie in cooperative ventures. The only question is whether such ventures should be organised by a single supplier or by groups of suppliers within the framework of a standards organisation.

Another example is the skills shortage that continuously constrains the progress of IT exploitation. That perennial factor is currently being aggravated throughout the western world by a demographic profile in which there are fewer young people to acquire the requisite IT skills. This shortage is yet further aggravated by the fact that existing skills are limited to a specific proprietary environment and all training that can be given in this situation must similarly take account of proprietary environments.

Finally, there are many past examples of innovations that could have succeeded had they not been tied to a small proprietary environment or relied on the resources of a single company to exploit them. ICL's content-addressable file store, and the Post Office's Viewdata systems, are just two that come to mind; no doubt the reader can think of many others.

IT has enough handicaps to overcome without handicapping itself in this way.

COST PERFORMANCE

As was pointed out in the explanation of what open systems are, a very great cost-performance advantage is required to justify a move between proprietary environments. The open-systems environment avoids this obstacle to progress.

Of more immediate significance is a fundamental change in the way small hardware systems are currently made. Traditional computer systems have conformed to what are now known as CISC (Complex Instruction Set Computer) architectures; however, in the last two years, a divergent technology known as RISC (Reduced Instruction Set Computer) has gained acceptance. What is of significance here is that RISC architectures offer considerable price-performance advantages for new machines. They also allow machine development to be faster and much less capital-intensive than has previously been the case, leading to the possibility of cost-performance gains for users and to the emergence of considerable innovation. However, for reasons stated above, this innovation is only likely to happen within the open-systems arena.

The other important aspect of cost performance concerns what is known as life-cycle costing. This focuses not, as in the past, on the cost of acquiring a system, but on the cost of owning it and operating it for its full life-cycle. This distinction is important because the loss-leader approach to selling is not unknown in the computer industry; it is quite possible for systems to have a low initial cost but a much higher cost through their whole life-cycle. This can be an attractive ploy where the sale is made in a relatively protected environment, such as a proprietary one, since the vendor makes the initial sale more easily and will probably get a good share of the full life-cycle costs over time. However, the practice makes little sense in an open environment.

There are a number of costs that are accounted for in life-cycle calculations (but not in acquisition ones). These include the cost of floor space, air conditioning and cooling requirements, maintenance costs (hardware and software), the cost of acquiring and training staff, etc. Clearly all these costs are likely to be lower in a truly open, competitive market-place.

THE SIGNIFICANCE OF THE PC

If all the above sounds fine in theory but you are sceptical about the practice, then look at your own use of computers. If you use a PC, you are probably already enjoying some of the benefits of open systems.

It is generally true, even if it sometimes seems unfair, that commercial decisions are rarely made on the basis of reasoning alone. A practical demonstration of a good idea is always more convincing. The rise of the PC is just that.

The PC market was around for a number of years before IBM produced its first personal computer. "DIY" machines were around from the mid-1970s; then came the Apple and the Commodore Pet, boosted by Visicalc and Wordstar. It is often said that it was not until IBM entered the market in 1982 that it attained commercial respectability; certainly, it was from that point that the market really took off. However, other key factors were the ability to clone the IBM PC, and the close similarity between PC-DOS (which was proprietary to IBM) and MS-DOS (which was not).

It was the openness created by these factors that provided the incentive for software developers to produce the mass of applications that quickly arrived. Prospective users could buy PCs from a variety of sources, with or without added services, at keen prices, and could similarly acquire software with a wide range of functionality at corresponding prices. This, above all, was a demonstration of the kind of market that openness can create.

The same phenomenon is in its early stages with regard to larger systems. As regards tools, it is already apparent in database systems; as regards applications, it is also apparent in office systems.

That is just the start of a trend that can only gather momentum.

The full breadth of applications is only just around the corner.

THE DREAM BECOMES REALITY

The dream promised by open systems is of a market freed of artificial barriers to change—one that allows truly free competition, resulting in optimum price performance and the highest-quality solutions for all. That dream is now in the process of becoming a reality. How quickly it arrives depends to some extent on how soon a critical mass of companies opts for open systems as a matter of policy. The evidence indicates that this day is drawing near.

An important side-effect of an open-systems market is that it should relieve IT departments of many of their frustrations in trying to respond quickly and flexibly to changes in business requirements. It holds the promise that applications can be put up quickly, chosen from the widest range of packages, ported from other systems or developed from scratch using any of the best development tools.

This in effect puts the users in control of IT. They are able to devise whatever strategies they require, unfettered by considerations of what is available from their particular supplier; they may use any supplier of open systems.

Above all, open systems promise to allow larger systems to incorporate the kinds of innovation and value for money that have been demonstrated as possible in the PC market.

4 The economics of open systems

There are certain ideas that apply to business planning and accounting that have particular relevance to open-systems thinking. The ideas do not derive from open systems but may be naturally associated with them. The purpose of this chapter is to describe them and their relevance.

The role of competition between enterprises as an incentive to innovation and a means of keeping prices in line with costs is well understood, and is mentioned many times in this book. It is key to the open-systems argument but needs no further explanation here.

Two further important ideas may be less familiar, however, and may need some explanation. These are planning for continuity, and a concept that is sometimes called opportunity accounting and sometimes called life-cycle costing; we will call it the latter.

BUSINESS PLANNING

One important input to business planning is what we have and know now. Clearly, financial plans draw on current accounting data as some basis for projections on costs and revenues. Professor Stafford Beer was keen on the idea that the immediate future is already largely shaped by decisions that have already been taken. If we knew which were the key decisions, how they were related and how they had been decided, then we would not need a crystal ball to foretell the future; a modelling system would suffice.

Proper business planning therefore depends on a detailed degree of knowledge of the current status of influential factors (*see* Figure 4.1). However, a simple extrapolation of trends from what is true

Figure 4.1   Business Planning: Getting Nearer To Where You Want To Be

today does not usually lead to an accurate picture of the future and certainly may not lead to the desired one. To suggest that it does implies that the future is totally beyond our control. Moreover, experience of business, particularly over the past two decades, suggests that discontinuities have a more important effect on the shape of the future than do any stable factors.

There is therefore a school of thought that proposes that business planning should start with a look at possible future scenarios, say five years ahead, and proceed backwards from there. In simple terms, a most likely scenario can be postulated and the business in question can define how it would like to be positioned within that scenario. When that position is defined, the focus of planning returns to the present to establish the present position in all relevant detail, and business plans are then drawn up to chart a course from the present position to the desired future one.

So what has all this got to do with open systems? The point is that planning purely on the basis of what we have now (largely proprietary systems) will not get us any nearer to the desired future. Extensions and extrapolations from environments which users are largely locked into cannot lead to open systems. To achieve open systems, we must plan to acquire them at points in the future and make assumptions (hopefully reasonable ones) as to when and in what form open systems of particular types will be available.

That process does not, of course, have to be done in a vacuum. As in the general description of the process above, once we have outlined a future role for open systems, we have to return to the present and assess what is available today, what is known to be under development and what are the probabilities of particular open solutions being available and when. We can then draw a "route map" of how and when moves to more open systems can be made. Unless we make those plans, we will not have open systems; they do not follow automatically from proprietary ones.

THE VEXED QUESTION OF VALUE

Attempts to justify IT systems on a global business basis, rather than on the basis of a local project cost-benefit analysis, have posed the question of the value of IT systems to the business. The most common business justification for IT systems in the past has

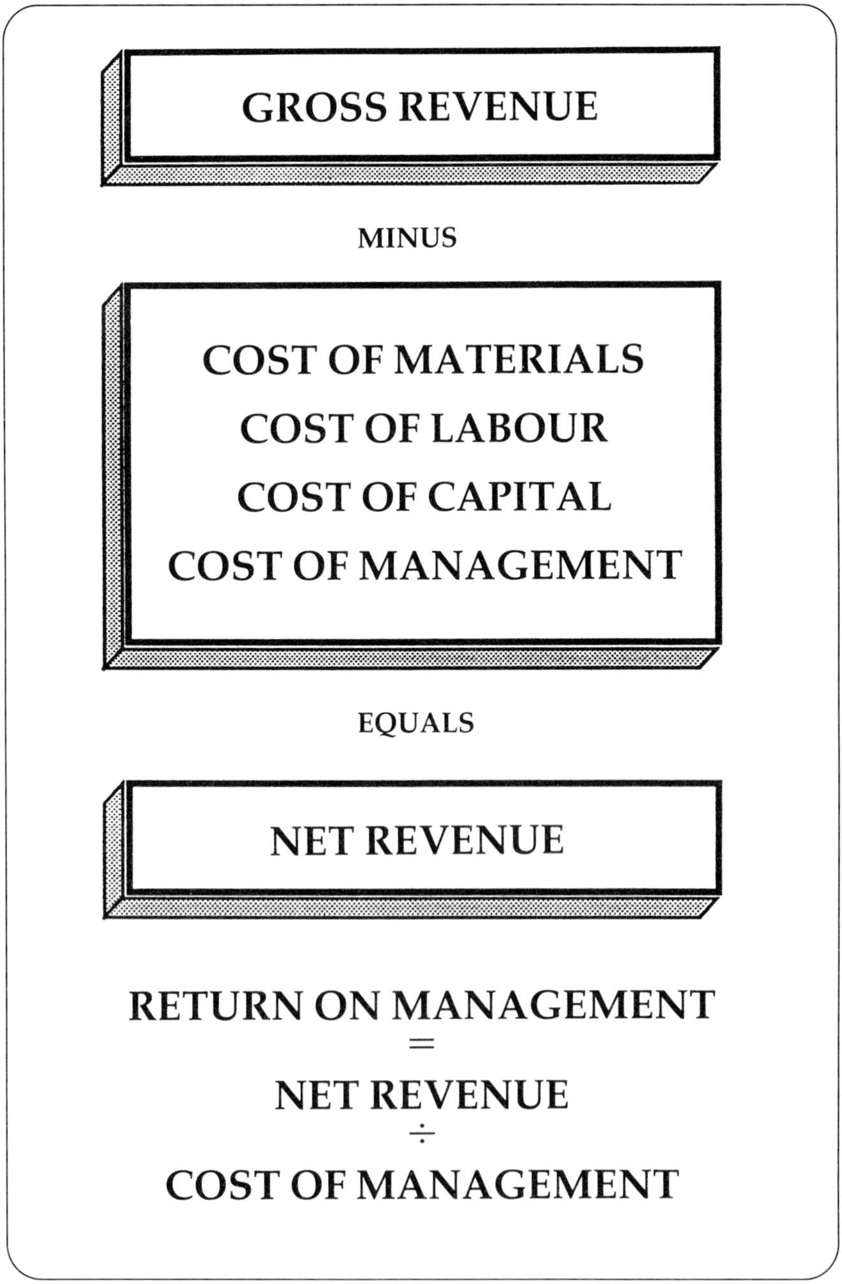

GROSS REVENUE

MINUS

COST OF MATERIALS
COST OF LABOUR
COST OF CAPITAL
COST OF MANAGEMENT

EQUALS

NET REVENUE

RETURN ON MANAGEMENT
=
NET REVENUE
÷
COST OF MANAGEMENT

Figure 4.2   Return on Management (Paul Strassmann)

been cost savings on, typically, headquarters or overhead functions. As the total spend on IT has grown, this basis has been challenged, and attempts have been made to give IT a more front-line role, aiming at competitive advantage and service innovation.

A less publicised direction is provided by Paul Strassmann's ideas (*see* Figure 4.2, Return on Management) about return on management as a more enlightening indicator of performance than the traditional measures of return on investment or equity employed. Strassmann objects to the latter on the grounds that they impute all value to capital; he proposes that capital should be regarded as a resource, like labour or materials, and accounted for at cost. Its value depends on how management uses it, and it is management in fact that is responsible for all added value. Hence return on management should be the key indicator of vitality.

Again, one can ask what all this has to do with open systems. The link is this. Systems aimed at providing a competitive edge typically have to be developed quickly and with a high degree of certainty that they will meet their schedules and perform as specified. Open systems, with their emphasis on building systems from standard components and with scalability as a key concept, provide a much better general basis for confidence than do proprietary ones. If a large part of the system can be built from proven components, then there will be fewer custom-built components presenting risk. If the original target processor begins to look inadequate as D-Day dawns, scaling up should present few problems and no large incremental cost. Moreover, the richness of the open-systems market-place will normally provide more options in the first place as to how the system can be built.

As regards return on management, the link is that IT is now the means by which most management information is delivered. For greater effectiveness, managers increasingly look to better information. Open systems promise greater flexibility and lower cost, both of which help to improve the return on management ratio.

LIFE-CYCLE COSTING

The practice that is becoming known as life-cycle costing is a reaction to the observation that decisions in favour of one system versus another are frequently made simply on the basis of the cost of acquiring a system. No account is taken of the costs involved in running, maintaining or enhancing the system, or indeed of other associated costs (*see* Figure 4.3). Advocates of life-cycle costing maintain that the estimated total cost of owning a system throughout its life-cycle should be taken into account as part of the acquisition decision. Since very few, if any, computer systems are acquired just as short-term, throw-away purchases, that seems a sensible argument.

An analogy with the debate over nuclear power stations may help reinforce this distinction. It seems that, on the basis of building a power station and generating electricity, nuclear power is a cost-effective option. However, the cost of disposing of nuclear waste in an environmentally acceptable way is expensive, and the cost of decommissioning a nuclear power station at the end of its useful life may well be prohibitively so. Taking all these factors into account changes the way we view the initial decision to go ahead or not.

The reason that this argument is important to open systems, lies more in the future than the present. At the current time, open systems are demonstrably cheaper in some sectors but more expensive in others. In the long run, however, it is obvious that open systems will be more cost-effective. The guarantee of freedom for competition that open systems bring with them in itself almost guarantees that. Other factors contribute to reinforce this long-term trend.

Stepping through the process of acquiring and using a computer system will help to illustrate this point.

Acquisition factors

The obvious acquisition factors, as noted above, are the price of the initial hardware configuration and of the software to be used. Several other factors should be taken into account, however, even at this early stage.

One factor is space. A computer system of any significance will have its own room, floor or building. The space required depends on the size of the equipment needed now and of any more

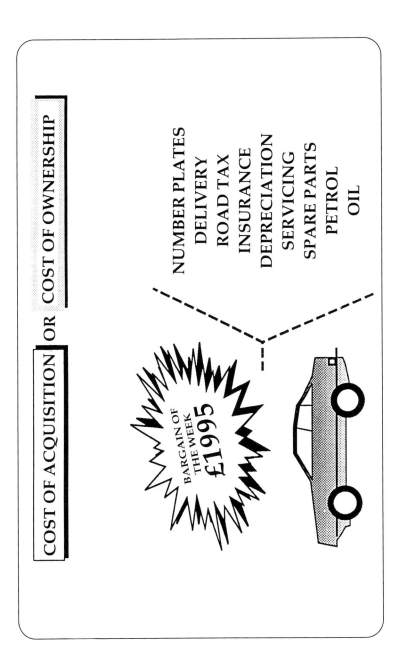

Figure 4.3   Cost of Acquisition or Cost of Ownership
Which Makes More Sense?

equipment that is likely to be acquired in the near future. It is common knowledge that computers of a given power get smaller every year, but it is not always realised that there are very significant size differences between systems of equivalent power at any one time. It is not just the size of the central processor that needs to be considered, but also the size of disks, tapes and network equipment. Buildings are expensive, and these costs are going up just as the costs of computers are coming down.

Environmental requirements are another factor. Does the system—again, not just the central processor but also the peripherals—need any kind of temperature controls or protection from dust, static electricity, etc? If so, what modifications to a normal office building have to be made? Does piping for water cooling have to be installed, for instance?

Power supplies are another factor for machines of any size. There is not just the cost of the power supply; machines that use more power will generate more heat that may have to be dissipated in some (possibly costly) way.

Software poses a different set of questions. Some suppliers charge for software according to the size of CPU that it runs on; some suppliers license software separately for each CPU, and also have licences to cover all CPUs at a particular site. In the case of PC software, it is often the user rather than the machine that is licensed. Some software is available on a rental basis, maybe even only on a rental basis.

Finally, there is the question of staff. Depending on the popularity of the hardware and software being installed, there may be a large pool of staff with the requisite experience from which to recruit, or there may be a very small one. The size of the pool in relation to the demand will be an important factor in salary expectations and in ease of recruitment.

Operational factors

Once the installation is up and running, the cost of maintenance comes into play. The price of hardware normally covers some period of free maintenance but the exact period can vary greatly between suppliers. Periods from three months to a year are common, and a good negotiator may extract even longer periods from an eager supplier. The price of maintenance also varies between suppliers, and can sometimes be bettered by third-party maintenance companies. Finally, there is the question of the quality of maintenance — an indirect but definite cost, which can usually be checked.

Software maintenance prices can vary generally in the range of 10% to 40% per annum of the original purchase price, with around 15% being the norm. Equally as important as the price is the quality of support and whether or not upgrades to the software are automatically included in the maintenance price.

Additions to the original system also present an opportunity for significant price variations. Being in "buying mode" is a permanent fact of life for large installations. Experience shows that all installations, whatever their size, tend to grow and grow rather more quickly than was originally envisaged. New acquisitions pose the same questions as the original ones, but with an added constraint: you are now locked into the environment that the original system operates under.

A proprietary environment that has only a relatively small user base may have a restricted range of devices and software outside the obvious offerings. That may not only pose the problem of lack of flexibility, but, more than that, it will mean that there is little or no price competition for the options that exist. Normally, that means you will pay more.

Upgrading factors

At some point, all systems reach "break points" in the hardware range or operating system being used. It may, for instance, be impossible to attach more disk capacity to a processor, or the acquisition of more terminals may require a different operating system or a different version of the existing one. The general questions here are the cost of the new processor/operating system and the ease with which the system can be converted to run with the new facilities.

In the case of most widely used ranges today, the cost of upgrading equipment should be no more than is reasonable for the extra processor power, disk space, etc. What is reasonable, though, in a supplier's terms is that the extra facility provided should offer equivalent or better value for money than the original configuration. If 20% more disk space is being added, the price should be no more than, and preferably less than, 20% of the price of the original disk configuration. This is reasonable in terms of the added value, but may be totally unreasonable in terms of the cost of the upgrade, which could be no more than an engineering "fix". Without the competition that an open market provides, there is no mechanism to force prices to bear a direct relationship to cost and to give the user maximum value for money.

The cost of conversion varies greatly both between suppliers and at different break points within any supplier's range. Additionally, if the software supplier charges by size of system used, additional software costs may be incurred even without any software changes.

If the user is locked into the supplier, there is nothing to be done except to be aware of these possible future costs when acquiring the system. The costs may turn out to be reasonable, but only competition in a free market-place can ensure that.

Decommissioning factors

Any computer system, like any power station, eventually comes to the end of its useful life. Typically, either the volume of the workload to be processed exceeds the capacity of the largest configuration in the machine range on which it is being processed, or else significantly more cost-effective technology has become available. In either case, completely new equipment, new system software and possibly even a rewrite of the application is required.

At the time a system is acquired, it is usually impossible to know either the date on which this eventual conversion will be needed or the costs that are likely to be involved. What is certain is that this time will come, and that in the past the cost of the conversion has been analogous to the cost of decommissioning a power station (to return to our earlier analogy); it has always been a large cost.

Where a proprietary environment is concerned, the actual cost depends on what is available from the supplier and the third-party market. In the worst case, where the top capacity of a range is exceeded, there is no solution at all available and the cost of converting to a totally different system must be incurred. However, suppliers have a strong interest in keeping their existing market base and so will usually endeavour to provide conversion aids to cater for other cases. The efficiency of these aids varies enormously, but the conversion is rarely simple or inexpensive.

Open systems offer only a partial solution to this problem, but at least they do offer a gain. Firstly, they ensure that any necessary conversion will actually be necessary and not arbitrarily imposed by the supplier; this entirely obviates the need for some conversions. Secondly, by providing an environment with the largest number of suppliers, they ensure that the best possible solution will be available from one source or another.

That is the most that can be done. Technology will (and should) advance over time, making older systems obsolete. However, even small or occasional gains on a typical system conversion cost are very much worth having.

DISCOUNTING TO PRESENT VALUE

Users wishing to adopt a life-cycle approach to costing acquisition alternatives may be content with a broad evaluation of the factors involved. Where a more formal, detailed assessment is required, account has to be taken of the value of money over time. Clearly, the amount payable for maintenance, for instance, two years or so ahead will effectively be worth less than the same amount of money today; inflation is one obvious factor. Most companies have some policy for calculating the value of money over time, and this will have to be brought into the evaluation.

The objective of these calculations, generally known as *discounting to present value*, is to arrive at a single figure for each alternative as a basis for comparing them. Even when there is only one option, the calculations may still be performed as a means of assessing the proposed change in terms of return on investment (ROI). Again, most companies have standard ROI targets against which to assess project proposals.

Discounting to present value thus allows concrete figures to be placed against life-cycle cost considerations, and provides a basis for evaluating alternatives and (if required) for comparison with general ROI objectives. At this point, alternative methods of financing the change—outright purchase versus some form of leasing or rental arrangement—can be brought into a final assessment.

SUMMARY

It is naive and simplistic to equate the cost of a system with the cost of acquiring it. Many of the costs involved in running equivalent applications vary enormously between suppliers. Although some of these costs may be unknown at the time a system is acquired, many of them can be known and others can be reasonably estimated. Adopting a life-cycle costing approach when making acquisition decisions provides a much more accurate picture of the cost of an application, and can often produce very large savings.

The short checklist provided below should provide a useful aide-mémoire for the more important considerations when systems are being acquired. Consideration should be given to the number of alternative sources of supply, as well as the cost, for each item.

LIFE-CYCLE COSTING CHECKLIST

Total cost of initial hardware:

— are lease and rental alternatives available, and if so at what cost?

— installation costs: computer room, environmental controls;

— number, cost and availability of staff needed to operate hardware;

— hardware maintenance costs over, say, four years;

— availability and cost of foreseeable add-on equipment;

— cost of foreseeable upgrades to CPU, disks, tapes over, say, the next two years;

— cost of networking to any other systems.

Total cost of initial system software:

- licence terms: CPU or site; purchase or rental;

- maintenance charges over, say, four years;

- cost of system software upgrades that are likely or will be necessary as a result of foreseeable hardware upgrades;

- cost and availability of systems programming staff.

Total cost of initial application software:

- initial licence and maintenance terms;

- availability and cost of foreseeable additional applications;

- availability and cost of application training.

Extra costs of staff:

- training costs not included above;

- availability and costs of contractors, consultants.

Estimated cost of decommissioning:

- is the application likely to exceed top-of-range capacity within, say, four years?

- if so, can information on the cost of conversion be gained from any source?

5 Standards organisations and standards

A trip through the relevant standards organisations is unfortunately likely to produce glazed eyes, and leave the reader baffled and bewildered rather than better informed. Nonetheless, a book on open systems should carry this information. It will perhaps help if the reader regards this information, apart from the introductory text, as reference material, to be used to locate sources as and when necessary rather than to be read through.

THE NUMBER OF ORGANISATIONS

The most bewildering aspect of standards organisations is their sheer number and diversity, and that of the resulting standards. This should not really be surprising, and once again an analogy may help.

The composition of a computer system is quite as complex as that of a large building such as an office block or a hotel. Brief consideration of the number of standards and associated organisations involved will produce a similar list. Not only are there general construction standards; there are also standards for most of the materials involved, standards for plumbing, insulation, lighting, sanitation, safety and for a host of other aspects of erecting and maintaining a building. Each separate aspect generally has a national association representing it, and often a separate standards body. The big difference in the case of a building is that most of the relevant standards are already defined.

To continue the analogy, a layman would find it just as baffling to grasp all the standards involved as he would to grasp all the standards relevant to computing. However, this is nothing like such a problem to building contractors, firstly because there are clearly defined demarcation lines between the different aspects of a building, which are dealt with by specialists who need know only their own part of the picture, and secondly because most of the products in such an established industry conform to the relevant standards.

No doubt, information technology will eventually catch up with the more established branches of industry. For the moment, what we can do to help is to make a few distinctions and demarcation lines in the IT scene to structure the information provided. What we will also do is to apply some editorial discretion, describing the major organisations and standards but omitting much of the detail.

Before doing that, let us first add a few words of caution.

THE LIMITATIONS OF STANDARDS

About ten years ago, in the dedicated word-processor market, it was fashionable to point out that a word-processing system had a "standard V24 interface", V24 being a commonly used standard for communications attachments. This statement was often used to imply that the system could communicate in a standard way with any other word-processing system or computer with a similar standard interface. That was not true.

The V24 interface defines little more than the number of pins and their positioning in a plug or socket. The scope of the standard does not include a definition of the type of information that each of the 24 lines involved should carry. One result of this was that a couple of suppliers created a niche market in little black boxes that identified exactly what was going down each wire. Along the way, however, a lot of users became sadly disillusioned with standards.

The point of this cautionary tale is that, if you believe a particular standard is important to what you are trying to achieve, you need to understand exactly what the standard covers. In most cases where this applies, either you will have a specialist who knows, or a little general questioning will reveal the required information; you merely need to take the point into account.

The second limitation of standards is that, for any given aspect of

IT at any one time, there may be more than one applicable standard. That is perhaps unfortunate, but getting the whole world to agree on any issue takes considerably longer than getting a usefully sized group to agree.

National standards, for instance, are typically agreed much more quickly than international standards in any field. That provides a less-than-satisfactory solution for multinational companies, but is certainly better than no standard at all. So it is with computer systems. Most users who seek to follow standards will choose particular sets of standards for particular aspects of a system. They will then seek suppliers who can provide system components to as many of their chosen standards as possible.

These limitations of standards are significant, but do not constitute a case against standards. Obviously, the more widely a particular standard is adopted, the more value it has for the user. However, following a standard adopted by just a group of suppliers leaves more options open than being tied to a single supplier.

IMPORTANT ASPECTS OF STANDARDS

There are a number of general aspects of standards that the user should be aware of. The comments which follow should shed some further light on their significance, and will also serve to explain some terms that the reader will certainly come across elsewhere. The five aspects to be considered here are *formal specification methods, conformance testing, reference models, functional standards* and *profiles.*

Formal specification methods

A standard, when defined, is usually expressed in ordinary natural language. Natural language is notoriously imprecise, and the specification of a standard, which must be interpreted accurately and widely, requires great precision. An answer to this problem is to supplement the relatively imprecise natural-language text with text in a formal specification language. The academic arm of the IT world is very interested in formal definition methods of many kinds, and much work is going on in this area. One or two formal specification languages are already around, and we will hear more of them.

Conformance testing

Precision is one problem, and marketing is another, that is tackled by conformance testing. Readers of this book may by now be persuaded that standards are a good idea. Marketing people are constantly on the look out for perceived "good ideas", and are often unable to resist the temptation to use the term "standard" to describe facilities that closely approximate to that ideal. Users who are misled by this kind of poetic licence tend to get rather irate, and are in any case entitled to some clearer guidance.

It is accepted in more established fields that a standard should be supported by a test, or series of tests, that demonstrates whether a particular product meets the standard. In effect, the tests are the most precise and complete definition of the standard. This principle is accepted in IT, but the tests are sometimes still lacking. The overall process, known as conformance testing, is quite critical to standards and, where conformance tests have been defined, users should ask their suppliers if their products are certified as conforming to the relevant standard.

A relatively recent illustration of the factors at play here is in the IBM PC-compatible market. Since the IBM PC was a de facto rather than a formal standard, there was never any question of formal conformance tests being created to prove or disprove compatibility. Nonetheless, since users needed to distinguish between real and supposed compatibles, the industry went in search of a solution. It turned out that a certain game called Flight Simulator exercised all the most critical aspects of compatibility, and this was therefore generally accepted as a kind of unofficial conformance test.

Reference models

If you have heard of a reference model, the chances are that it is the OSI reference model (Figure 5.1) that you have heard of. In fact, there are many more.

The idea of a reference model arises from the realisation that creating standards in an unsystematic way over any given field can create more problems than it solves. This relates to the point made earlier about the scope of a standard. Ideally, before any attempt is made to produce standards in any given field, an

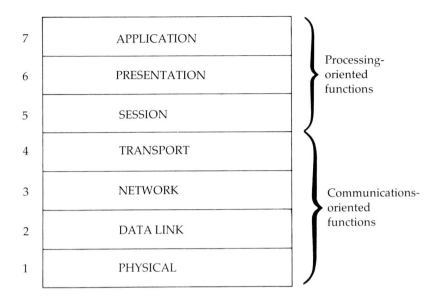

Figure 5.1   The 7-Layer Reference Model

overall structure for (or model of) the field should be defined. A decision can then be made as to the scope that each standard within the field should have, so that the whole field can eventually be standardised without there being any overlap or conflict between the standards. A model that defines a field of endeavour in this way is known as a reference model.

One problem with IT is that it is too new, and is changing too rapidly, for any generally accepted reference model of the overall subject to be feasible. However, it is possible within the current state of the art to identify some areas of IT that can usefully be isolated and subjected to a coherent process of standardisation. Networking is one example, and has resulted in the OSI reference model. Reference models have also been defined (or are being defined) for electronic document interchange (EDI), computer graphics, data management, open distributed processing and information systems engineering. Reference models are intrinsic to the standardisation process, and these models will in future guide the creation of standards in the fields they delineate.

Functional standards

The term "functional standards" implies that some standards are

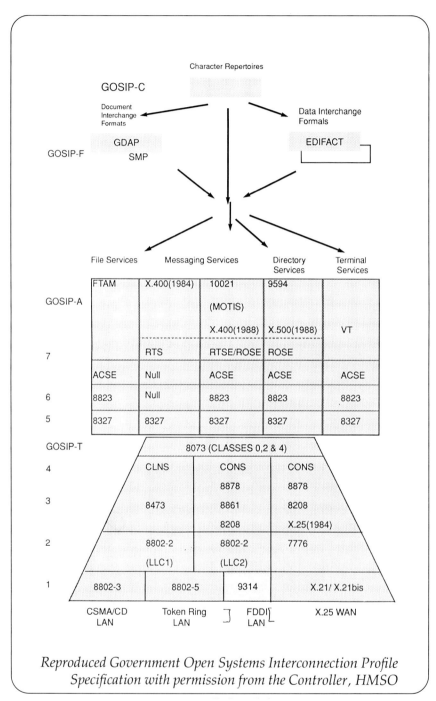

Reproduced Government Open Systems Interconnection Profile Specification with permission from the Controller, HMSO

Figure 5.2   GOSIP V3.1 Architectural Model

not functional, but that is not the distinction involved here. The problem is this: standards should cover all useful possibilities within their scope; but in a very diverse and complex field such as networking, the number of options that a standard must include can render it virtually useless to suppliers who must confine themselves to a practical size of product set, or to users who wish to interconnect a fairly small set of common products.

The answer to this problem is to create a functional standard, which defines a subset of the whole standard, or a recommended concatenation of separate standards, to cover a specific common case. For such cases, which may cover 90% of most users' and suppliers' concerns, only the functional (rather than the full) standard need be considered.

Profiles

Profiles are a little difficult to explain, since they are somewhat arbitrary. However, the concepts explained above will help. Essentially, a profile is a set of functional standards that defines the implementation of an integral part of a reference model. It can be thought of more simply as a concatenation of functional standards. The most likely context in which the term will be met is with reference to GOSIP, which stands for Government OSI Profile: a set of functional OSI standards defined by the government for use in its installations. See Figure 5.2.

TYPES OF STANDARDS ORGANISATION

In line with our definition of open systems in the first section, we need to distinguish between three principal types of standards body.

Firstly, there is the national or international, quasi-governmental type of standards organisation: the British Standards Institution (BSI) is the obvious, if not the most relevant, example of this type.

Secondly, there are some alliances of suppliers who decide that definition of some standards is in their common interest: the Open Software Foundation (OSF) is an example of this type.

The third type is not so much a standards body as a set of standards effectively created by suppliers who have achieved such a market share as to create de facto standards: IBM's network architecture SNA and Microsoft's PC operating system MS-DOS are both in this category.

Within our definition of open systems, all of these types of standard or standards bodies are relevant. Purists might suggest that only the national and international bodies really count, but the objective of this book is to be useful rather than pure. National and international standards may carry more weight in the long run, but the type of organisation involved also typically takes longer to get a standard agreed. Users cannot wait years for decisions that have to be taken today; a standard from any source that carries a large enough user base (and hence investment), and that can be acted on now, is often better than no standard at all.

These three types of standards body, together with the relevant areas of application, are used in the notes below to provide a reference list and a structured snapshot of the major standards that are relevant to open systems. Prepare for abbreviations and acronyms!

FORMAL INTERNATIONAL ORGANISATIONS

The major formal international organisations concerned are the Joint Technical Committee 1 (JTC1) of the International Standards Organisation (ISO) and the International Electrotechnical Commission (IEC), which are United Nations (UN) agencies; and the Consultative Committee for International Telephony and Telegraphy (CCITT), which feeds into the International Telecommunications Union (ITU), which is also a UN agency. ISO is made up of representatives from each national standards organisation, the British Standards Institute being the UK member. CCITT is similarly made up of members from each nation but, in this case, they are the national PTTs, British Telecom being the UK member.

JTC1 has 16 subcommittees formed into four groupings, and two further groups that do not have named subcommittees. The total of six group(ing)s is as follows:

— Advisory Group;

— Equipment and Media Grouping;

— Application Elements Grouping;

— Systems Grouping;

— Systems Support Grouping;

— Special Group on Functional Standardisation.

We won't go into the subcommittees. Among the major standards that are being developed within JTC1 are OSI, POSIX, IRDS and SQL. All these are explained in the section on major standards below, so we won't go into them here.

The role of CCITT is to facilitate the operation of international telecommunications networks and it therefore overlaps with ISO/IEC JTC1 in the area of computer networking. Where this overlap occurs, there is generally (mercifully) an agreement between the two bodies to work cooperatively to produce joint standards. This sometimes results in different "labels" for the standards defined but the same definition: CCITT X.125, for instance, is the same as ISO 8326.

FORMAL NATIONAL ORGANISATIONS

United Kingdom

There are a number of UK organisations concerned with standards in different ways. With respect to IT, they generally feed information into the international bodies and make internationally agreed results available, rather than creating standards themselves. Some of the major bodies are listed below:

The British Standards Institution (BSI) is the most useful source for the text of agreed and draft standards. It sells these at generally low prices, depending on the size of the text. It is the official UK body on the International Standards Organisation (ISO).

The National Computing Centre (NCC) is similarly a source of information on standards, having an advisory service and several publications of its own on standards.

The Institute of Electrical Engineers (IEE) is the source of many national electrical standards, and overlaps with IT in this respect. It also has a good library and a number of its own publications.

The British Computer Society (BCS) is in a sense the equivalent to the IEE that is concerned with IT specifically.

Finally, the IT Standards Unit of the Department of Trade and Industry is a further source of information. In particular, it publishes a list of OSI-compliant software.

United States

The USA has counterparts to the UK organisations listed above. Because of the predominance of US-designed systems throughout the world, these often have a quasi-international influence. The major organisations are as follows:

The American National Standards Institute (ANSI) is the US equivalent to the BSI, and has an equivalent role. It has been particularly active in language standardisation.

There is no direct equivalent to the NCC, but the National Institute of Standards and Technology, formerly known as the National Bureau of Standards, fits generally in its place.

The Institute of Electrical and Electronic Engineers (IEEE) is the US equivalent to the IEE, and has in particular been responsible for originating the POSIX standard and some local area networking standards.

Finally, the US equivalent to the BCS is the Association for Computing Machinery (ACM).

Copies of most US national standards can be obtained quite quickly through the British Standards Institution.

ALLIANCE ORGANISATIONS

88open is a group of major suppliers that have agreed to produce software that maintains binary-level compatibility with the Motorola 88000 chip series.

COS (Corporation for Open Systems) is an association of users and suppliers that promotes open systems and specifically provides test scripts for OSI conformance testing.

DISC is an organisation created to promote the use of standards in IT among UK enterprises.

ECMA (European Computer Manufacturers' Association) is a consortium of computer manufacturers, originally those in Europe but subsequently joined also by the Americans. It makes recommendations to various formal standards organisations.

EISA is a group of PC suppliers, including many of the major IBM-compatible suppliers, seeking to perpetuate and extend in a standard form the original bus architecture of the IBM PC.

EurOSInet is a European consortium of over fifty suppliers of IT products and services concerned with demonstrating the practicality of OSI solutions.

OMG (Object Management Group) is an organisation funded by a wide alliance of suppliers that aims to promote the practical standardisation of object-oriented systems. It does this by making recommendations and publishing a book of interface specifications for modules that have already been created.

OSF (Open Software Foundation) is one of two rival groups (see UNIX International) of suppliers seeking to define standard versions of UNIX. The groups are not mutually exclusive. OSF was formed before its rival UNIX International by IBM, Digital and many other major computer suppliers.

OSITOP is a user group that provides a channel for user recommendations to the OSI standardisation committees.

OSNMF (Open Systems Network Management Forum) is an alliance of suppliers that is seeking to bring network management products that conform to international standards into the marketplace more quickly.

Uniforum is not strictly a standards body, but more of a standards information and promotion organisation; its board consists of representatives from major suppliers.

UNIX International is the other group of suppliers (see OSF) seeking to define standard versions of UNIX. This group is based around the originator of UNIX, AT&T.

X/Open is dedicated to the development of an open, multivendor Common Applications Environment (CAE) based on de facto and international standards. Essentially, it brings together standards established by other bodies to form various necessary environments, and publishes the collection of standards that define the environment in the form of a guide. It has published guides on portability and security.

SOME MAJOR STANDARDS

A list of all relevant standards would easily fill the rest of this book, and would serve little purpose; details of all standards can be obtained via the relevant standards organisation. This section simply provides a handy reference to the major standards that you are likely to come across in incomprehensible form (eg X.400) in the general literature. With the help of the section below, you should in most cases have an idea of what is being discussed.

CAE: Common Applications Environment is a concept created by X/Open to describe a set of standards covering operating systems, languages, networks and data management that will enable applications to be ported between systems.

EDIFACT: A proposed standard for electronic document inter-change (EDI) that is being developed by ISO.

Ethernet: A standard for local area networks (LANs) that originated in work carried out by Xerox; it is now internationally standardised as IEEE 802.3 or ISO 8802/3.

FDDI: Standing for Fibre (Optic) Distributed Data Interface, this is an international standard for data transmission over fibre-optic cables.

GOSIP: A set of functional standards for the application of OSI standards in government installations, both in the UK and the USA (see *Profiles*, p41).

HDLC: Stands for High Speed Data Link Control, and refers to a commonly used transmission protocol defined in the second layer of the OSI model.

IEEE 802.3: See *Ethernet* above.

IEEE 802.5: See *Token Ring* below.

ISDN: A standard defined by CCITT for the transmission of voice, computer data and facsimile data in digital form over normal telephone lines.

LU6.2: A proprietary protocol developed by IBM within its

Systems Network Architecture (see *SNA*) to perform basic peer-to-peer connections.

MAP: Manufacturing Automation Protocols is a set of standards for production automation, as its name implies. It was developed originally by General Motors in the USA, and relates closely to the OSI model. It received acceptance because it was available before equivalent OSI implementations.

MS-DOS: A proprietary, rudimentary operating system developed by Microsoft for personal computers. The very large majority of PC application programs being used today run under this operating system.

OS/2: The operating system developed by IBM for its second wave of personal computers, the PS/2s. It is much more fully functional than IBM's PC-DOS (a derivative of MS-DOS), and competes with UNIX in the PC/workstation market.

OSF/Motif: A standard for the user interface to a PC/workstation, proposed jointly by Hewlett-Packard and Microsoft, and adopted by OSF.

OSI: Open Systems Interconnection is the overall term used to describe the standards already defined, and still being defined, by ISO/IEC to allow disparate systems to intercommunicate.

POSIX: The IEEE standard (1003.1) for interfacing between an applications program and the operating system, particularly UNIX.

RS232C: A commonly used standard, defined by ANSI, and used to connect computer processors to low-speed peripherals.

SAA: IBM's proprietary architecture for software development and portability of applications between IBM platforms; it stands for Systems Applications Architecture.

SNA: This stands for Systems Network Architecture, and is effectively IBM's proprietary version of OSI—limited to IBM systems, but with gateways to OSI networks.

SVID: System V (UNIX) Interface Definition; see *UNIX* below.

TCP/IP: Transport Control Protocol/Internet Protocol is a networking standard developed by the US Government Department of Defense for use in its networks. The definition of the standard, and the implementation of products that met it, proceeded faster than OSI. So it has been adopted by some commercial organisations as an interim standard until OSI catches up. It approximately covers the functions of levels 3 and 4 of the OSI reference model.

Token Ring: The IEEE standard for local area networks using token rings for the control of communication; technically defined as IEEE 802.5 or ISO 8802/5.

TOP: Technical and Office Protocols is a set of standards designed originally by the Boeing company in the USA for office systems. It can be linked closely with MAP, and has received considerable acceptance because it filled a vacuum.

UNIX: The proprietary operating system developed by AT&T that has been adopted by open-systems vendors as the standard operating environment for machines of workstation power and upwards. Standardisation is based generally around Version 5 of UNIX, known usually as System V.

V24: The CCITT standard for plug/socket connections between computer processors and peripherals; it corresponds approximately to ANSI's RS232C.

X.21: The CCITT standard for communication between user devices and a circuit-switched network.

X.25: The CCITT standard for communication between user devices and a packet-switched network.

X.400: The CCITT standard for store-and-forward networks, which generally provide the networking backbone for electronic mail and office systems software.

BINARY COMPATIBILITY

What is a binary program?

The language a program is written in is called the source language and that will typically be a language such as COBOL, Basic, C, or a 4GL. The source program is then compiled into object code, which is also sometimes called semi-compiled or relocatable binary. This form of the program is then linked to other modules, library routines, etc before a final transformation into executable form. The binary compatibility discussed here refers to this final, executable form of the program.

Characteristics of binary programs

This final form of the program has a number of characteristics that are significant from either a user's or a supplier's point of view.

Firstly, since all that has to be done before a program is run is to load it, once it has been demonstrated to work it will always work. Where programs are held in some form other than the final, executable form, there is always the possibility that a different compiler, different library routines or some other difference in the compilation process will cause it to fail in a given instance, even though it has worked before.

Secondly, since the final form of the program effectively hides the logic to all except the machine, changes to the logic or privacy of the code are very difficult. That characteristic is primarily of benefit to the supplier but also protects the user's investment.

Thirdly, the program still needs the operating-system services in order to run, so compatibility at this level is dependent on the operating system being the same when it is run.

Fourthly, the program will run on only one instruction-set architecture. In the past, this has effectively meant only one machine or machine range. More recently, however, many machines from a variety of sources, particularly PCs, have been built using the same basic chip. This provides the same underlying instruction-set architecture.

Finally, there are two further dependencies for complete compatibility at this level. The first is generically known as system dependency, and consists of technical hardware characteristics such as the precise timing of the CPU clock, bus and so on. It was differences in characteristics such as these that caused some clones of the original IBM PC to fail to be recognised as perfect clones.

The other dependency is on the exact peripherals, particularly terminals, used with a system. For a program in executable form to run with a normal VDU and a dot matrix printer, for instance, it must necessarily have details of these embedded in it, and will not run unchanged with, for example, a Prestel receiver and a laser printer.

These two dependencies require another standard alongside binary compatibility if true compatibility is to be achieved.

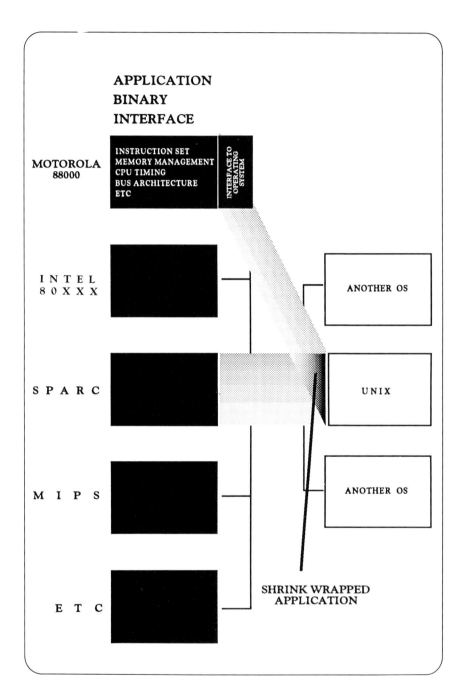

Figure 5.2   Shrink Wrapped Applications

APPLICATION BINARY INTERFACES

As indicated above, the idea of a binary compatible standard is that it should allow a program supplied in executable form to run on any CPU with a given instruction set under a given operating system. Binary-compatible standards are generically known as application binary interfaces (ABIs) and there are currently several of them, one for most of the major commodity chip sets, all designed to interface with UNIX. ABIs exist, for instance, for the Motorola 68000 and 88000 chip sets, for the MIPS chip set, for the Intel l860 chip set and for the SPARC-conformant chip sets. Figure 5.2 illustrates an ABI example.

ABIs have essentially three elements. Firstly, they define a number of limits on the use of the instruction set: data types, page boundaries, error codes for particular conditions, etc. Secondly, they define basic clock-timing and memory-management features: the basic CPU functions associated with the instruction set. Thirdly, they define the interface to any operating system the CPU is to run under, so that system calls to operating-system functions and library routines can be made in a standard manner. Essentially, an ABI should be able to apply to any operating system for which an interface corresponding to the ABI is written; currently, the operating system in question is UNIX.

In the case of UNIX, the ABI may, for instance, define a set of system calls sufficient to call all UNIX functions conforming to the POSIX and SVID standards, and a set of system calls to access a library of supplier-dependent features, so that suppliers may exploit particular features of their own system.

These last two points need some further explanation. One of the problems with cloning IBM PCs, mentioned earlier, was that the cloners had no idea which system features were important to compatibility and which weren't. They therefore had to reproduce every feature as closely as possible. The system calls to UNIX functions mentioned above effectively define those UNIX functions that are critical to compatibility, thus overcoming this problem.

As regards supplier-dependent features, a criticism of standards in general has always been that the decision-making process of standards bodies is too slow to allow progress in ideas and technology to be reflected quickly in implementations. The provision of system calls to supplier-dependent features allows suppliers to incorporate enhancements in systems, provided these are not critical to the running of the program. That is, suppliers may incorporate useful features that embellish a program, provided the program will run adequately without them.

In the case of the Motorola 88000 ABI, the way this is implemented is through a library of routines identified by a supplier ID. Access is made to only those routines that have the ID of the machine in question at any particular time. Thus the extra features will be made available if they apply to the machine being used, and will simply be ignored if they do not (in which case other features may be available). This allows the incorporation of non-critical machine-dependent features without thereby constraining the program to be run on any particular machine.

Finally, the question of peripheral dependence is passed on to the operating system to resolve. UNIX defines terminal-independent I/O routines that everybody already uses. Instead of these being tied in the program to specific peripheral devices, they are linked to a database of peripheral details, and run-time calls build terminal-specific commands on the fly. A similar process, using the X-Windows graphics standard, covers the problem of incompatible graphics hardware.

Still on the agenda

There are some areas in which current ABIs need further development, and of course it can be assumed that more ABIs will be developed in future for other chip sets. One area for attention, for instance, is object file formats for object (or semi-compiled) code; this would extend the relevance of the ABIs to programs originally written for non-conforming systems, providing a means of importing partially linked programs into a given ABI environment. Another is network-based applications.

Summary

The whole idea of ABIs is to enable software houses to provide users with a stream of easy-to-load applications that will run on all systems running a common CPU and operating system. In short, to provide users with ease of use and flexibility. The ultimate usefulness of an ABI therefore depends on large numbers of important software houses supporting it. Indeed, in most cases software houses themselves have been instrumental in getting ABIs defined. All ABIs have groups of software houses aligned behind them.

6 Compatibility and portability

In this chapter we will try to convey some of the key ideas and issues behind compatibility and portability. Probably the most fundamental point to understand is that both are very much a matter of degree; defining either is a similar task to defining the length of a piece of string.

Compatibility and portability are similar in that both describe the ability of systems and programs to work together. Compatibility is generally used to describe this property from a systems point of view, portability to describe it from a program point of view.

In essence, compatibility between systems means that two systems can be connected, or replace one another, as components of some larger system, without the user needing to customise interfaces or change any other components of the larger system.

Few systems can meet this criterion exactly; compatible systems meet it inexactly, but for all practical purposes. The ultimate key to the degree of compatibility between systems lies in assumptions as to what "all practical purposes" are, and the rough edges will be found most commonly in the treatment of exceptional conditions (particularly errors).

The same points apply to portability. A portable program will run on different systems, if subjected to any necessary automatic transformations (generally compilation), in exactly the same way for all practical purposes. Any rough edges will be a function of the assumed practical purposes and exceptional conditions.

It has been normal to think in terms of source programs with respect to portability; hence the qualifying clause above, allowing the need for recompilation between systems. More recently, with the advent of commodity chip sets, portability is often achieved at the level of run-time code, giving rise to software which is generically termed "shrink-wrapped"; you just unwrap it, load it and go. The ability to do this is a result of binary compatibility, which was described in detail in the preceding chapter.

A GENERAL PARADIGM

A good analogy to the problem of portability and compatibility is the problem of writing a recipe and cooking instructions for arbitrarily different circumstances. Let us assume we need to make a beef casserole, with potatoes and some green vegetable, and our job is to write the instructions. That is an apparently simple task, fulfilled every day in various magazines and newspapers. Its simplicity, though, is very much dependent on a form of standardisation—what we can very reasonably expect the reader to know and to have available. Computers, as ever, are different.

A typical recipe will start with a list of ingredients, on the bland but valid assumption that these will be simply acquired from a shop (or freezer). In the case of a truly general-purpose program, we could (perhaps whimsically) question this assumption and include some instructions about killing a bull, waiting for market day or searching the local countryside for suitable vegetables.

Assuming we have the ingredients, we then have to describe how to cook them. A normal recipe will simply state the temperature and length of time (Gas Mark 6 or 360°F for one hour), based on assumptions of standard appliances. However, suppose we attempt to describe the same process for someone with a camp fire and two billy cans, another person with two electric rings in a bedsitter, and yet another person with a fully-equipped modern gas kitchen. Suppose we have to describe the process in minute detail, as programs do.

You can, if you wish, attempt for yourselves a description that will fit all circumstances. You will not manage it. How do you describe the process of obtaining heat? Do you light a match (for an electric ring)? Do you turn a switch (for a camp fire)? Do you heat three saucepans simultaneously (on a two-ring electric stove)? Where do you suppose that water is obtained both in a modern kitchen and by a camp fire?

What you will quickly realise is that the more detailed your description of the process to be performed, the more you have to know about exactly what appliance is available to the user. It is possible to write a very general description that applies to all the different circumstances (ie a program that is portable), but only if the appliances being used are essentially similar or we can easily supply alternative versions for different circumstances.

We could, for instance, disregard (for all practical purposes) the very minor differences between different makes of four-ring gas stove. We could also write the recipe in two halves, one providing general instructions and the other consisting of several sets of specific instructions for each type of cooking appliance we wished to consider. The recipe needed in any one case could then be "consolidated" by combining the first half of the recipe with the set of cooking instructions relevant to the specific cooking appliance in question.

For a collection of recipes for an international readership, we might also have to consider different languages (French, German, etc) or dialects of the same language (eg British "tap" versus American "faucet", or French "quatre-vingt dix" versus Belgian French "nonante"). This is similar to the necessity in computing to take account of different source languages (COBOL, Basic, C, etc). These language differences add an extra dimension to the translation process.

That, in a nutshell, is the problem of portability. Each different system that a program is to run on requires, potentially, a different version of the program, because the program must take account, in its most detailed form, of the specific hardware it is running on. Each different original language will also require translation facilities. Each translation and/or different version of a program equates to extra cost. Incompatibility, at the end of the day, is an economic rather than a technical problem. It is always technically possible to make the various necessary translations, but only at very significant expense. The problem then becomes one of how to avoid these translation costs.

REDUCING THE COST OF INCOMPATIBILITY

It should be evident from the above discussion that all problems of portability and incompatibility would be solved if we all used one language and one type of machine.

That is not possible at the moment, since we currently use a wide variety of languages and machines—nor would it be a desirable state of affairs to seek. There are good technical and economic (and hence business) reasons why languages and machines should differ—reasons to do with efficiency, effectiveness and the legitimate role of innovation. However, what we should seek, and what is gradually happening, is the gradual reduction of incompatibilities to the usefully necessary minimum.

Standardisation, in various forms, is the principal process contributing to a reduction in incompatibilities. The general way in which this is happening is discussed briefly below. There is also a technical concept that is important to this process, and we will describe that first.

THE UNIVERSAL VIRTUAL MACHINE

Many years ago, when the "standard" (ANSI) Fortran language was suffering from the emergence of several hundred dialects, there were people who ran what were called Fortran laundries. These laundries would identify all the dialectal variations from the standard in a program and "launder" them out. That was one of the first general attempts at improving the portability of programs between systems.

Around twenty years ago, another idea gained proponents. The idea arose as a possible efficiency gain on the need for a separate compiler for each different language to be used on each different machine. If there are four different machines and four different languages to be considered, then sixteen (4 × 4) compilers must be developed. The idea was to introduce an intermediate level between source languages and machines, translate from source languages into this intermediate level and translate from the intermediate level onto specific machines. This would reduce the number of compilers that had to be developed to eight (4 + 4, not 4 × 4).

The crux of the technical problem was to design a suitable intermediate level, between all relevant machines and languages, that would provide compilation efficiency comparable to that of conventional compilers, so that the proposed gains could be realised. This intermediate level was generically known as a compiler-compiler language, and two early attempts at it were Uncol (Universal Compiler Language) and BCL (Basic Compiler Language). In the event, neither managed to define a level of description that allowed the necessary compilation efficiency; machines were simply too different.

The significance of these developments lay in their attempts to define an intermediate level between source languages and machines. The intermediate level at which the old compiler-compilers operated is in essence a definition of a universal virtual machine. That idea has now become current again and has implications for open systems. The idea failed originally because the population of machines to be considered included too many very different architectures. Given a smaller number of machines to consider, or machines that are more alike, the idea could be valid. In fact, it is basic to IBM's SAA.

SAA is still much more theory than practice, but effectively defines a set of conventions into which source programs can be mapped and from which object code can be generated to run on a small set of IBM machines with different architectures.

Theoretically, any programs that meet the prescribed conventions could also be used to generate code for a set of machines from any other supplier, if the necessary compilation facilities were made available. Thus SAA compliance could in principle be used by any supplier as a de facto standard from which to develop compilers for his own machines. As has already been said, SAA is still more theory than practice, but the potential is there for SAA to be used in this way.

Perhaps of more immediate significance is that, through a variety of types of standard, machines have become much more alike since the early compiler-compiler days.

BENEFITS OF STANDARDISATION

We will not repeat here all the major standards initiatives, and the benefits thereof, described elsewhere in this book. Here are just some of the more important points.

At the lowest level, the majority of systems are now built from a small number of (commodity) chip sets: the current Intel, Motorola, MIPS and SPARC-conformant chip sets, for instance. This provides a much greater degree of uniformity at the instruction-set level than has ever been present before. Alliances of suppliers supporting these chip sets, aimed at providing binary-level compatibility, reinforce the uniformity.

At the operating-system level, the continuation of MS-DOS and the effective focus now on only two variants of UNIX adds yet more uniformity. At the source-language level, the emergence of C, a language specifically designed with portability in mind, reinforces the trend to uniformity in software. And SAA is likely to become a very significant de facto factor.

These items do not in themselves come near to a single universal system, but they do serve to reduce the cost and increase the potential efficiency of the translation process for very large ranges of programs and machines.

To this must be added the effects of the standards bodies that are gradually defining more and more interfaces within and between systems. Technically, these do not greatly affect the internal similarity of systems, but they do have an impact on interoperability and also in defining the boundaries that any translation process has to work within. Where different components exist to meet a standard interface, the translation process can cease and it will suffice to consolidate the relevant component into the program at run-time.

7 Migration to open systems

Few companies will have the opportunity to take a "green fields" approach to open systems; most will have to move from existing, proprietary environments. So even when the arguments in favour of going for an open-systems strategy are accepted, there still remains the question of how to effect the transition.

The most suitable means of migrating to open systems will depend on many factors: the type of system involved, whether a new or existing application is being considered, and the financial policies of the company concerned are just some of them. Most companies will have to take a gradual approach, moving individual or small groups of applications at a time to more open environments and piecing together a new infrastructure. During the period of transition, means will also have to be found to enable open and proprietary environments to coexist for a while.

It would be difficult to cover every situation, but the discussions below should provide pointers to the solution of most common cases.

Since all major suppliers now include some open systems in their product portfolios, it is also always worth consulting your current supplier for suggestions. Suppliers that can no longer keep their users locked into a proprietary environment will nonetheless be keen to maintain their customer base, and may offer trade-in or financial incentives. Take care, though, to ensure that the open systems offered really are open and not another proprietary environment with an open label on it (see Chapter 13: *Choosing a Supplier*). At least your current suppliers, more than anyone else, are likely to be aware of the specifics of migrating from their proprietary environments to open systems.

PLANNING FOR MIGRATION

It shouldn't need saying, and probably doesn't in most cases, but any company would be foolish to jump or drift arbitrarily into open systems. A plan of migration will be needed, and a corresponding schedule of actions must be drawn up to fulfil the plan. If you fail to plan, you effectively plan to fail.

There is little point in describing this process in detail here, since it is essentially no different from planning and implementing any other project. The specifics that apply to open systems are dealt with below. Anyone who has managed an IT project, particularly anyone who has installed a system, will be familiar with the general disciplines involved. Anyone without that experience will find numerous books on IT project management that will provide the necessary background.

THE BEST AND WORST CASES

Firstly, let us dispose of the easy cases. For any new stand-alone application, or any application system that is scheduled to be totally written off and replaced, the solution is simple: acquire an open-systems version. The sole "conversion" cost may be the cost of some staff retraining, which is likely to be minimal since only the staff who manage the installation (ie those who have anything directly to do with the operating system) will be affected.

If the application is not entirely stand-alone but needs to communicate minimally with other systems in the company, a fairly simple communications link could provide the answer. Many installations already use packet-switching links between systems of disparate architectures, taking advantage of the OSI standard. Precisely what kind of link will be most suitable is difficult to define in the general case, but there is a wide choice of simple links within the OSI framework.

Secondly, let us deal with the most intractable cases. These will be where an application has been written in-house for a specific machine. It is likely that neither the programs nor the associated files will be easily portable onto another system, so the user may have to contemplate the full costs of a total rewriting of the application. In these circumstances, many users will opt to stay with the existing system until it reaches the end of its useful life.

There are two corollaries to this. If the application has been written in a popular language such as COBOL or BASIC, it will be worth investigating how closely the version of the language on the existing system resembles the version on the proposed new system. If the differences are very minor, conversion may not be too costly.

The other corollary concerns maintenance costs. In general, the cost of maintaining a system increases in real terms over time. With hardware, the relative cost of newer technology is the major factor. Hardware price performance improves generally by about 20% per year, so that by the time the hardware is fully written off, the annual maintenance charges will approximate to the purchase price of a new system of similar power. With software, repeated changes over a period of years (to correct errors, allow for changes in system software, revise the application in line with company and legislative changes) exact a toll in making the software less efficient, more complex and more fragile. At some point the company will have to weigh the projected cost of continuing maintenance against the cost of replacing the system. That review of ongoing costs should be, but is not always, a regular process. Open systems provide an extra reason to review such costs in the light of new alternatives that promise greater cost-effectiveness over the system life-cycle.

PC INTEGRATION

A good place to start is with the integration of PCs, since they, more than any other type of system, demonstrate the characteristics of open systems. Also, many companies currently have to review their PC policies and requirements in the light of 80386 and 80486 machines, and the consequent relevance of the UNIX and OS/2 operating systems at this level.

The first essential is to be clear about requirements, so we will dispose of the trivial cases. If all the integration you need is to be able, for instance, to share a peripheral or two (eg a laser printer, a scanner or a plotter), then a simple switch will normally meet this requirement at very low cost. Similarly, if there is a very local need to be on-line to send telexes, faxes or other forms of electronic mail, then a single PC equipped with communications facilities may meet the need; there is no point in creating any kind

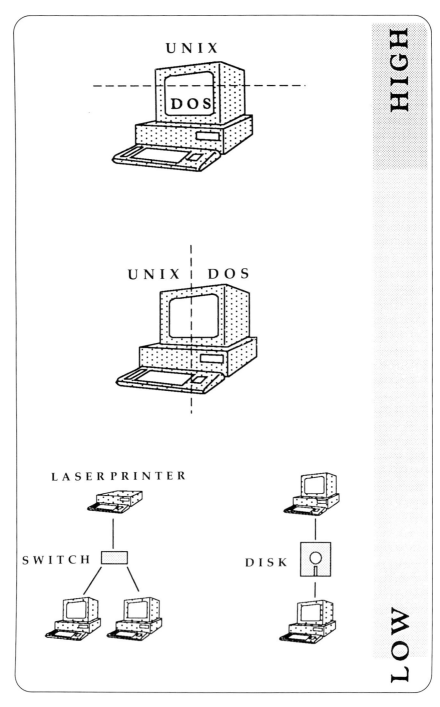

Figure 7.1   Degrees of PC Integration

of network. In other cases the simple passing of disks by hand within an office or between adjacent offices will be appropriate.

The only reason for mentioning these cases is to stress that one must start by being clear about the requirement. Integration is not an absolute term but a matter of degree, and greater degrees of integration will normally cost more (and also deliver more). Large organisations are likely to require a high degree of PC integration in most cases.

Integrating DOS

Most PCs will currently be running DOS (PC-DOS or MS-DOS) and it will take a long time for all the well-loved DOS applications to be ported to UNIX and OS/2. It is therefore a safe bet that DOS will be around for a considerable time yet. So it is going to have to coexist with UNIX and/or OS/2 and/or any other mid-range operating system that may be around the company in question.

The obvious way to enable DOS to coexist with another operating system— UNIX, for instance—is by some form of emulation. The emulation may be effected in hardware or software, although the tendency is increasingly towards software emulation. Care should be taken to distinguish between the ability simply to emulate DOS under UNIX and the ability to integrate DOS and UNIX on the same machine.

In the former case, UNIX or DOS programs must always be run in isolation from one another. In other words, to switch from a DOS program to a UNIX program, the DOS program must be terminated, the files closed and then the UNIX program started up. The user must always be aware of which operating system is running at any one time.

In the latter case, UNIX and DOS programs can be running simultaneously, allowing data to be passed between them and making the operating system running at any one time transparent to the user. It is this integrated form of emulation that will in general be most desirable.

Local area networks (LANs)

Physical interconnection between PCs is most likely to be effected by the use of one type of LAN or another. The most commonly used standards for LANs are Ethernet (IEEE 802.3), Token Ring (IEEE 802.5) and Starlan. A LAN provides the facility for passing data and programs between the PCs and peripherals attached to it. The first LAN to gain general acceptance was Ethernet, devised originally by Xerox, with Starlan following as a derivative; Token Ring gained rapid acceptance once it was adopted by IBM.

A further component of this technology is the LAN operating system, which is needed to control the LAN. The two most commonly used are Novell's NetWare and Microsoft's LAN-Manager.

LANs have often been installed on a local ad hoc basis, much in the same way that PCs originally crept into companies. Large companies, particularly those that have had LANs for some time, are therefore quite likely to have more than one type of LAN already installed. Fortunately, that should not pose too many problems for integration.

The most obvious difference between the different types of LAN is that each involves a different type of cabling. It is not possible, therefore, to change the type of LAN simply by changing the software installed. The good news is that fibre-optic cabling, conforming to the FDDI standard, is decreasing in cost, gaining rapid usage and can support any current type of LAN.

So, what would be a reasonable strategy for bringing LANs into line with an open systems policy? Firstly, fibre-optic cabling should be used for new LANs if at all feasible; this leaves the most options open. A further step is to standardise, as far as possible, on a single LAN operating system. Which of the IEEE standards the individual LANs conform to is then of less significance.

The linking of LANs together or into a wide-area network can be achieved by means of a bridge or a router. The distinctions between these devices are not relevant here.

Is it always cost-effective?

It is more straightforward to apply an open-systems policy to PCs now than to some other aspects of IT because PCs already display many of the characteristics of an open market-place. PC systems are ubiquitous and growing rapidly in power and functionality. They appear to be such a major factor in IT systems overall that it may seem strange to question their long-term significance.

Nonetheless, there are some largely unquestioned assumptions in the "PC revolution" that are worth a moment's thought.

Let us consider some of the factors that have contributed to the widespread use of PCs. There are many opinions on the key factors, but some or all of the following are generally agreed.

Firstly, there was price. Professor Hoare of Oxford University once described the objective of a time-sharing system as being to give every user the illusion of having their own PDP-8 (an early, minimal Digital system). PCs offered users their own system at a price that fell within the bounds of operational rather than capital budgets.

Secondly, there were easy-to-use applications that had wide relevance. One view is that it was the use of spreadsheets by executives that primarily sold PCs; enthused by the capabilities that first Visicalc and then Lotus 1-2-3 gave them, they not only spread the word among their peer group but also readily sanctioned the purchase of PCs by their staff. Word processing (initially in the form of Wordstar) and simple database applications (via dBase) extended the domain of routine applications.

The price performance of PCs with basic software shattered the markets for number-crunching minicomputers and traditional accounting equipment, for dedicated word processors and for semi-mechanical filing systems. Quite simply, PCs replaced them.

The result in larger organisations has been a proliferation of single-user systems acquired for specific individual purposes over time. The current move, as described above, is to integrate these PCs into larger IT systems. However, the result of integrating PCs can deliver what looks very much like a traditional multi-user minicomputer system, but at a somewhat higher cost. A LAN serving a group of users and sharing applications and peripherals among them essentially does no more than a minicomputer with multiple terminals. PCs may be the cost-effective solution for individual users, but are they necessarily the best solution for groups of users carrying out similar work?

The economics of technology at any point in time underlie this question. PCs came in originally because they provided a powerful individual facility cheaply. Now that everybody has one, to what extent do they still need to be individual facilities? If the cost of terminals with, say, four megabytes of memory and a central server (CPU and disks, running X-Windows) is less than the cost of an equivalent PC and LAN configuration, shouldn't the PCs be replaced by terminals? Diskless PCs, as these newer kinds of terminal are becoming known, are already around, and provide grounds for rethinking the role of PCs.

There is a good analogy in the traditional way of connecting PCs to mainframes. Normally this has happened on a project-by-project basis, each involving small numbers of PCs, and the solution has been to use communications boards (typically Irma boards) in each PC. This is usually a good solution for small numbers of PCs, but may not be cost-effective if a group of projects is considered together; in that case, typically if 50 or more PCs are involved, a central hardware or software alternative may provide better cost-effectiveness.

The point is that solutions that are cost-effective for individual or small groups of users may not be so when the number of similar users reaches a certain critical mass. Local, short-term decisions of cost-effectiveness can prove uneconomic over time, and such decisions should be subject to periodic revision. Simple extensions of current decisions may not lead to the desired future (see Chapter 4: *The economics of open systems*).

MIGRATING MID-RANGE SYSTEMS

In the case of mid-range systems, when we talk of migrating to open systems we are talking of migrating to UNIX. UNIX is no more similar to any proprietary environment than proprietary environments are to one another. So what has to be contemplated is in essence similar to a switch between proprietary environments. The major differences are that it may be possible to retain much of the hardware, and in the best cases many of the files. Also, there is a good chance that this will be the last major conversion exercise that the company will have to contemplate for a considerable time.

A point that should have been checked when the move to open systems was planned is whether all current and foreseen applications are available to run under UNIX. For the most common applications, the only problem is likely to be one of choice. More specialised applications will have to be checked out.

The key to the degree of effort and expense required is going to be the portability of the application software involved. Users generally cannot afford to think in terms of porting applications themselves. Software houses can, though, and have done so increasingly over the last five years or so. Many have opted to write applications in C, the most favoured language for portability. Software suppliers who have decided to go for the UNIX market (and that is the large majority) have tended to port the same package to as many different systems as is feasible. Where possible, packages originally written for a proprietary environment have been ported to UNIX, rather than the package being rewritten.

This is important to users because it means in some cases that conversion to UNIX may involve little more than acquiring the UNIX version of the package. Existing files, which could absorb considerable conversion effort, will not need to be converted. Additionally, there will be no need to retrain staff using the application, since the software will look the same to them. It should be mentioned, however, that an application written originally for some environment other than UNIX may run less efficiently under UNIX, and may lack some features of the original version because of dependencies in the software on the original operating system or target machine.

MIGRATING TO OPEN NETWORKING

Networking is intrinsically complex and therefore so is the subject of migration to open networks. There are many books covering this subject in detail; the following provides just some basic points and suggestions.

The first distinction that must be made clear, for those new to networks, is that between the physical and the logical network.

The physical links between nodes, terminals, etc, be they copper wire, fibre-optic cables or microwave links, are generally neither OSI, SNA nor any other architecture (though LAN standards have some cabling dependencies, see Figure 7.1). The same is

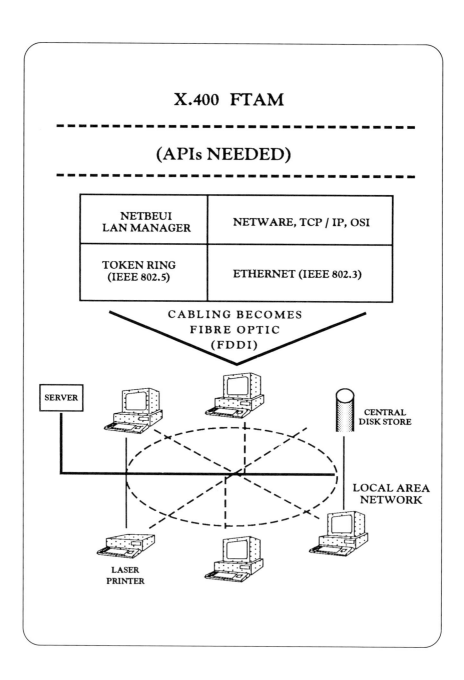

Figure 7.2   LAN Integration

true for almost all devices within a network. These are all components of the *physical* network.

Communication between devices across the network is achieved generally by software which conforms to a set of protocols; the protocols must be the same at each end of the communication to ensure that commands, messages, etc are interpreted correctly. The software is part of the *logical* network, and the protocols are OSI, SNA, TCP/IP, etc.

Today, most devices in a network are programmable, and many are provided with alternative software that incorporates one or another set of protocols. There are also a large number of packages on the market, generically known as protocol converters, that accept one set of protocols as input and generate another set of protocols as output. These can, for instance, intercept signals from a device that does not conform to SNA protocols and convert them so that they appear to the device that receives them to come from an SNA device.

These points are fundamentally important because they mean that any physical network could be either OSI, SNA, TCP/IP or conformant to any other protocol. Moreover, different parts of a network can conform to different protocols, and even the same parts of a network can use different protocols for different purposes, at effectively the same time. In practice, relatively few networks of any size conform to purely one set of protocols; these are sometimes known as "vanilla" SNA (or OSI) networks.

There is always, however, a dominant protocol for the major structure, or backbone, of the network. This is most often proprietary, such as IBM's SNA or Digital's DECnet; if it is an open network, the backbone will conform to the ISO X.25 protocol. Realistically, it is not feasible to migrate this backbone gradually; at some point, there has to be a decision to stay with the existing proprietary backbone or switch totally to X.25.

So what might an open systems migration strategy for networks look like? At the LAN level, the general objective is to provide a transparent transport mechanism. The major open option is to use some version of Ethernet with TCP/IP or NetWare (which is set to become OSI-compliant), with Token Ring and LAN Managers as the principal alternative.

As yet, no standard application programming interfaces have been defined to sit above this level, and they are needed. All the user can do at the moment is to try to ensure that the code accessing this transport layer of the communications network is isolated as far as possible in separate program modules. When APIs are defined, it will only be these modules that will need changing.

As regards higher-level protocols, there is still much that needs defining and/or implementing in the open-systems world. However, FTAM and X.400 provide a basis for electronic mail and file transfer for the moment; other facilities are on the way.

A SMALL EXAMPLE

Here is an example of a possible small step in the direction of open systems, but one that may apply quite generally.

Suppose that a company has a major transaction processing application, written a decade ago (and patched regularly since), running under a mainframe operating system. It could, for instance, be a CICS application running under MVS. The requirement is for a considerable amount of management in-formation, the data for which is locked up in the TP files.

The mainframe solution would be to use a 4GL or report generator to create the necessary application on the mainframe.

However, the cost of a 4GL on the mainframe looks high, and the mainframe is already creaking under the load placed on it by the TP application. Upgrading the mainframe or porting the TP application are options that are also ruled out on the basis of cost.

Given a policy of moving to open systems, this would be an opportunity to start in that direction. A solution would be to place a UNIX "stub" on the mainframe, which should be a minimal extra load on it. The stub would be used to extract from the TP system the data needed for management information, and to download that data onto a PC or a small minicomputer running a relational DBMS under UNIX. The application would then be written on the PC/mini, possibly using the same 4GL that could have been used on the mainframe, but acquired (since it is a PC/mini version) at much lower cost.

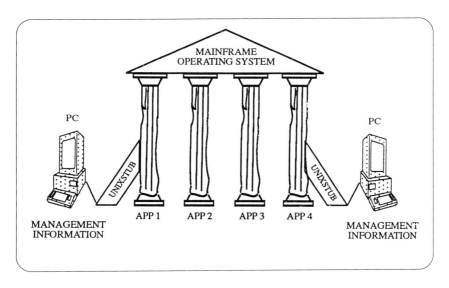

**Figure 7.3   New, open applications can be
built around old, fragile applications**

The result should be a useful application, implemented cost-effectively, and a small step towards open systems, without any disruption to the major business systems. The latter, of course, remains a problem to be tackled sooner or later, but one that can wait until the economics of conversion versus continuing maintenance dictate a change. See Figure 7.2 to illustrate this.

8 UNIX

UNIX is at the very centre of open-system developments for machines ranging from large PCs up to powerful minicomputers. So it is worth spending a little time understanding where UNIX came from, its current status and likely future developments.

THE EARLY DAYS

UNIX was originally designed and implemented around 1970 by Ken Thompson, a software engineer at AT&T Bell Laboratories, for use by people like himself. This point is important because it explains the initial strengths and weaknesses of UNIX.

UNIX is conceptually very well designed, with layers of functionality carefully separated and a consistent command format. This is not visible to users of applications running under UNIX, but is an important aspect of the operating system for system developers. Other important strengths of the original UNIX were that it is a multi-programming operating system and has good communications facilities. These are in fact the kinds of strengths one would expect from an operating system designed by a software engineer to facilitate his own work.

UNIX's original weaknesses derive from that very fact. It was weak on facilities to handle commercial files, had poor security and assumed only one processor (a Digital PDP-11). UNIX did not have these facilities because a software engineer did not need them for his own workstation.

A supposed weakness of UNIX is its user interface, which is generally described as "unfriendly". This is a half-truth which illustrates the danger in the term "user-friendly". The way the term is used often implies that all users are the same; obviously they are not. What is friendly to any particular user depends on what he or she is used to or what seems natural to him or her. The UNIX user interface is certainly unfriendly to most people who are likely to use applications running under UNIX; but then they should never be interfacing directly to the operating system. The target user of UNIX was the software engineer, to whom the interface is likely to be very natural indeed. In its proper context, the UNIX user interface is a strength, not a weakness.

Nonetheless, it would have been difficult to predict the success of UNIX from these relatively unambitious beginnings. What changed that was its rapid acceptance among software engineers who came across it, which led AT&T to make licences for it available to academic and scientific institutions at a very low price. A direct result was that colleges produced an ever-increasing flow of software engineers who had used UNIX, liked it and wanted to take it with them. Since UNIX was written in C, a high-level language that was relatively easily portable, it could be ported without too much effort (provided a C compiler was available) to whatever hardware the software engineer used next.

Thus UNIX spread rapidly through its target market but did not appear significantly on the commercial scene until the early to middle 1980s.

THE COMMERCIALISATION OF UNIX

Through its hold on software engineers, UNIX moved into the scientific/industrial areas of commerce as the major operating system for workstations. That moved it out of the groves of academe into industry, but not into commercial data processing.

That move came with the burgeoning of the market for commercial minicomputers in the period around 1980–1985. The main hardware suppliers all had a relevant machine or two to offer, but system houses bundling computer systems and applications together were making more and more of the sales. A typical offering of the time would be a Digital PDP-11 of some sort, CDC disks, Pericom VDUs, Centronics printers, perhaps a set of integrated ledger applications, and the RTSE operating system. RTSE was perhaps the major operating system in this market, but it only ran on the PDP-11. What was needed was an operating system that ran on many different ranges of minicomputers.

The solution turned out to be UNIX. Its first acceptance in the commercial market-place was as an "engine" to drive small to medium-sized computer systems. That, after all, is close to what it was originally designed for. Add its portability, its acceptance among software engineers (who were building the applications to run on the minicomputers) and its relatively low cost, and you had a winner.

THE STANDARDISATION OF UNIX

One of the strengths of UNIX—its portability—also turned out to have a serious disadvantage. It was available in source-code form, and a number of organisations bought the source code and proceeded to modify it. The result was a large number of variants: in particular, the Berkeley campus of the University of California developed a variant (BSD) that became used quite widely; IBM and Digital developed their own versions, AIX and Ultrix; and Microsoft developed Xenix. It began to look as though there could be more major variants of UNIX than there were major proprietary environments. That was not a positive direction for a proposed universal operating system to take (Figure 8.1).

If UNIX was ever to become in any sense a universal operating system, the challenge was to inhibit variations and encourage convergence on a standard version. This process began seriously when AT&T produced an interface definition for its UNIX Release 5, known as System V. The interface is generally known as SVID (System V Interface Definition). Release 3 of System V effectively absorbed Xenix, and Release 4 did the same for the Berkeley variant.

Both of the main alliances to form a standard UNIX, UNIX International (UI) and the Open Software Foundation (OSF), accept System V and SVID as a base point. A third (and important) factor came with the formation of X/Open, a consortium independent of UI and OSF that was formed in 1984 to define practical UNIX standards from the best of the UI and OSF proposals. X/Open publishes a *Portability Guide* that describes these functional standards.

Three further moves along the path towards a universal operating system must be mentioned. Firstly, AT&T wanted to distance itself as a supplier of UNIX, so placed it in a separate company

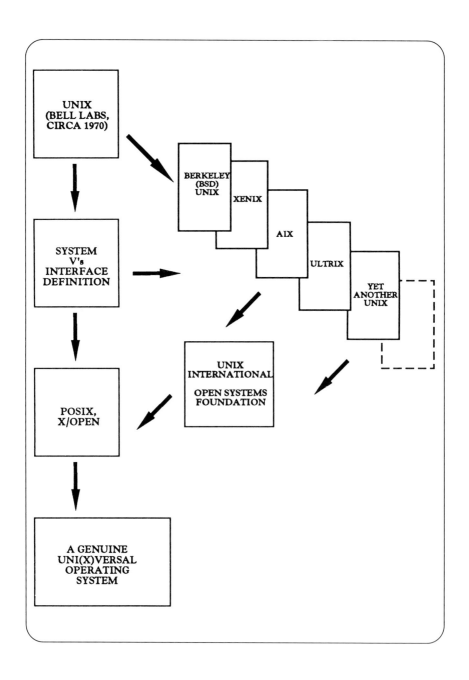

Figure 8.1   UNIX: Divergence and Convergence

called the UNIX Software Operation (USO); it has offered shares in the company to other suppliers. Secondly, IEEE produced a standard known as POSIX which defines a set of necessary interfaces to a (universal) portable operating system (see Figure 8.2). The POSIX standard is based on UNIX, but does not specify the AT&T code. Thirdly, OSF is engaged in defining an architecturally neutral distribution format (ANDF) for UNIX applications. Conformance and ANDF would allow the direct translation of any such application from the form designed for one version of UNIX to the form required by another.

Where does all that leave us? In fact, it leaves us quite close to our goal. At the time of writing, UNIX International appears to be gaining ground over the Open Software Foundation, thus resolving one source of conflict. Software developers are tending to look to POSIX for features they can rely on as being stable, and X/Open is subsetting practical standards along the way. The practical situation emerging is that POSIX will define the general standards, with major input from UNIX International, from which X/Open will subset the functional standards.

Eventually, POSIX may define a set of interfaces that makes the operating system transparent to applications. That would allow greater innovation in operating-system design, and would also allow new applications written to the POSIX interfaces to be free of operating-system compatibility considerations for ever. UNIX may disappear, or become just a discernible trace, evidenced by occasional characteristics, in a different operating system altogether. Provided backward compatibility is maintained for the time (and to the extent) that is necessary, the possible disappearance of UNIX won't matter at all. For the moment, however, we will return to some of the previously mentioned weaknesses of UNIX and discuss these.

TACKLING THE WEAKNESSES

As indicated above, the weaknesses of UNIX generally stem from the origins of its design as an operating system for a software engineering workstation. The design principles of UNIX are very sound; it is the scope of the facilities it takes into account that is too narrow in a general commercial environment. Because of UNIX's clear design, adding the lacking facilities is not a major problem.

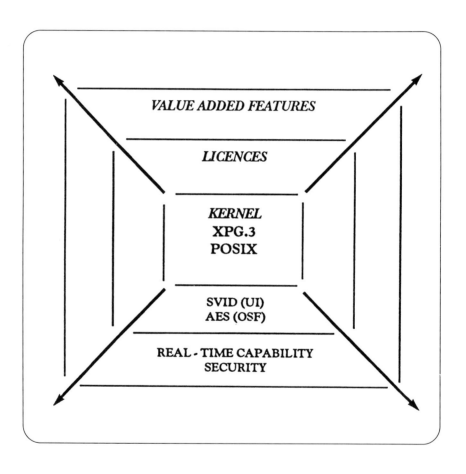

Figure 8.2   UNIX Standardisation

Such has proved to be the case in practice, to a large extent. The addition of commercial file-handling facilities was perhaps the earliest shortcoming to be tackled. The original UNIX did not recognise records within files, neither did it have any access methods. All commercial software developers know how to produce the routines to provide those facilities, so that short-coming presented few problems.

Lack of security was more of a problem, but that is now the subject of standardisation activity.

Lack of power, particularly for large-volume on-line transaction-processing (OLTP) applications, which are now common, also creates more difficulty. However, that has now been tackled successfully for the large majority of companies. To an extent the problem can be resolved by "throwing more iron at it" (ie more powerful hardware). However, it does remain a problem for the moment for the few companies that require a very high throughput of transactions. Those applications typically run today under the IBM MVS operating system using the IMS system software, and will remain a minority challenge for UNIX (or a POSIX successor) for some time to come.

The lack of system utilities is already being countered, and appears to be a very temporary problem. The lack of instrumenta-tion is probably a reflection of the relatively small machines that UNIX has so far been run on. In fact, rudimentary resource-monitoring information is already obtainable via fairly obvious "hooks". The problem is that the user has to write routines on a DIY basis to pull off the monitor records and convert them into a format suitable for performance/capacity management. However, resolution of that problem really only requires an official pronouncement as to which hooks are standard, plus a market base of large UNIX systems of a sufficient size to interest instrumentation suppliers.

Finally, there is the problem of UNIX's assumption of a single processor driving the system. The assumption was reasonable at the time UNIX was designed; modern systems, however, typic-ally derive their power from multiple processors. Resolution of that problem involves rewriting the kernel (the very heart) of UNIX, but this has already been done by several suppliers (by Data General in its DG/UX, for instance, Figure 8.3). Effectively, it

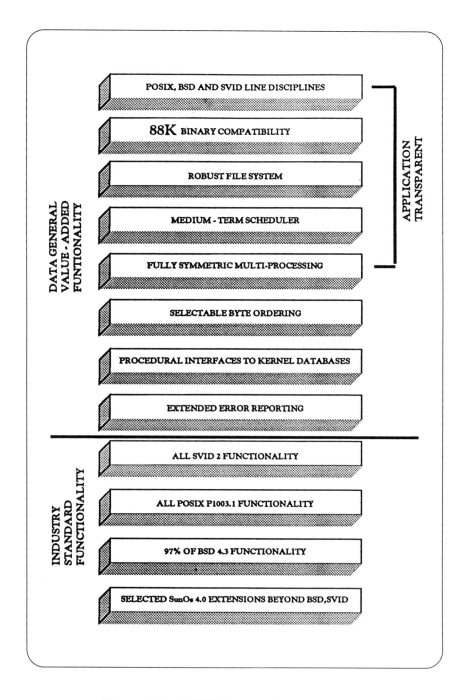

Figure 8.3   DG/UX Kernel Functionality

allows UNIX to drive very much more powerful modern "engines".

So not only can all the shortcomings of the original UNIX be resolved, but most of them already have been. The outstanding problem is that the original shortcomings have generally been resolved by different suppliers at different times in different ways.

THE PROBLEM OF DIFFERENT "FLAVOURS"

As indicated above, the pristine clarity of the universal UNIX message is clouded by the existence of various "flavours" of UNIX. As also indicated above, clouding the message is all they should do; the message is still there, and valid. However, it is perhaps worth looking at where the differences in flavour come from, and suggesting what users might do about them.

Broadly, the real problem comes from history and from the inherent weaknesses in the standards-creation process. History creates problems in that most suppliers have started with early and different versions of UNIX and wish to preserve this early investment. Much current UNIX code, therefore, accounts for efforts to provide upward compatibility between early UNIX versions and UNIX System V Release 4. What that means to users is an overhead—an operating inefficiency—entailed through the use of this code. Any version of UNIX that did not carry this code would be more efficient but less universal, and therefore less generally acceptable as a standard.

An inherent weakness of the standards process, as noted elsewhere in this book, is that agreement between several parties takes considerably more time than agreement within one supplier. Also, subsequent implementations of the standard are likely to create inefficiencies in mapping from a general standard to a specific system. Individual suppliers can make decisions faster and take account in those decisions of what can be implemented most efficiently on their specific systems. What the UNIX standards bodies have done, as a compromise, is to create a number of standard interfaces to allow suppliers to exploit the strengths of their individual systems up to, but only up to, certain defined interfaces. This is a compromise, but defines useful levels of compatibility whilst allowing some freedom to innovate and provide added functionality. See figure 8.2.

The different flavours of UNIX are unlikely to disappear totally for a long time, if at all. However, the nature of them will change over time. The process can be thought of in terms of a gradually expanding concentric set of squares or circles. At the centre are the standards defined by POSIX and XPG/3; these will be extended over time to include facilities in the outer areas. Next come the licensed versions of UNIX, available from USO or OSF, which are the basis of virtually all suppliers' versions of UNIX. Finally there are the proprietary extensions that most suppliers add to differentiate their product and give it greater appeal in the market-place.

The above items can be counted as acceptable clouds that slightly reduce the clarity of the message. Unacceptable clouds are attempts to tie UNIX, one way or another, to a single proprietor. The following section provides some guidelines on sorting out the former from the latter.

SOME CRITERIA FOR OPEN VERSIONS OF UNIX

Not all of the following criteria will apply in every situation, but they form a general guide to assessing the "openness" of any supplier's version of UNIX.

First, it is worth considering the interface between UNIX and the various ABIs (application binary interfaces) available for commodity chip sets. Since this affects the ability to use "shrink-wrapped" software, it is as well to know which ABIs interface cleanly to the version of UNIX you are considering.

Secondly, upward and downward compatibility may be important to you. Which previous versions of UNIX is the version in question compatible with? And does the supplier have a track record of taking compatibility into account? It should be noted that compatibility is something of a two-edged sword in that it inevitably involves some inefficiencies in the code. However, in any move to a more open environment, such inefficiencies are generally a reasonable price to pay, and may be less than the eventual cost of being locked into a "proprietary open" environment.

Thirdly, how interoperable is the version of UNIX in question with other suppliers' versions running on other machines? This is essentially a question of the distributed computing protocols (eg file transfer, office-system functions) available with it, particularly TCP/IP and OSI protocols.

Fourthly, scalability is usually an important consideration. It should be possible to run any version of UNIX on processors of widely different power. A little care is needed to avoid pushing this point to extremes; very small PC configurations and very large mainframes are unsuitable vehicles for UNIX at the moment (and indeed may always be). However, UNIX can encompass a range from the more powerful PCs (eg 80386 and above) to high-power mid-range systems or small mainframes.

Finally, any prospective purchaser will inevitably look at the value-added functions all suppliers use to enhance and differenti-ate their version of UNIX. Different functions will appeal to different users; the point to note in this context is that all such functions should be separated from the UNIX core by suitable interfaces, so that programs may make use of them but are not locked into them.

SUMMARY

When the goal is universality, variants and shortcomings are not good news. Certainly, it is generally true at the moment that many of the major proprietary environments can compete with UNIX in terms of functionality and efficiency. In the short term, they can also compete on price, if not on breadth of choice.

In the longer term, as was pointed out in the discussion of the standardisation of UNIX, divergences are rapidly being elimin-ated. The latest variances tend to be minimal, and all the signs are that the speed of standardisation is increasing. The major vendors committed to open systems see lack of standardisation as a brake on the market, and are anxious to have inconsistencies resolved as soon as possible.

Given that, and the demonstrable viability of UNIX, via POSIX, as a universal operating system, there seems to be no case for choosing any operating system other than UNIX as a mid-range system strategy. Short-term requirements to choose another environment must take account of the probable higher long-term costs of sustaining that system over its full life-cycle.

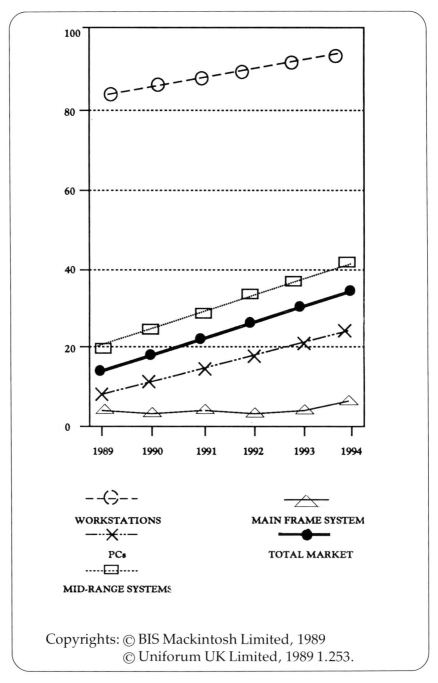

Figure 8.4   Penetration of UNIX in the Hardware Market

A recent survey by BIS Mackintosh, in conjunction with Uni-forum UK, of UNIX penetration of the market bears out the points discussed above (see Figure 8.4). In 1988 UNIX alone increased its percentage market share in the mid-range sector; all proprietary environments lost ground to it. BIS Mackintosh projections show it doubling its market share in all the relevant sectors over the next four years, leaving it with around a third of each sector and a gathering "bandwagon" effect. Development teams base their product planning on market intelligence such as the BIS Mackin-tosh survey, and aim at the largest market share. With the exception of the large mainframe sector, the critical mass is clearly going to be with UNIX, and that is where the development teams are putting their money.

9 Software availability

Availability of software is one of the most important aspects of the viability of any system. In the general commercial case, no matter why a system was originally acquired, an installation will use a number of types of software over the system's life-cycle. Application packages, software development tools such as a DBMS and a report generator, a procedural language or two, and probably some system utilities (eg for archiving, dump/restart), will all usually be necessary.

When looking at software availability, we therefore need to distinguish between the various types of software and satisfy ourselves at the outset that likely future requirements, as well as initial ones, can be met. It helps if there is not only a reasonable choice of software to meet each need but also a reasonable choice of potential suppliers.

Since general availability and wide choice are specific goals of open systems, we would not expect there to be a problem. However, it is still early days for open systems and the problem of locating what is available still needs discussing.

In this chapter we will also look at the availability of software of each type within specific environments, as primary sources differ in each case. We will not attempt to list packages, since there are tens of thousands that may be relevant; rather we will enumerate the major sources.

The principal environments to be considered can be grouped broadly into PC/workstations, small-to-medium multi-user systems, mainframes and networks. It should be noted, however, that in particular cases it may be important to have the same package running in more than one of these environments.

Without listing individual packages, it is impossible to indicate to which software this applies. Suffice it to note that most suppliers of widely used packages are working to develop versions that run on multiple platforms, and many have already made significant progress. The answer in any given case may be in one of the sources listed; if it is not, then ask the supplier.

PC/WORKSTATION ENVIRONMENTS

The principal environment of interest in the basic PC market is that provided by MS-DOS and its IBM derivative, PC-DOS. There are literally tens of thousands of applications packages, tools, utilities and basic communications facilities available.

It would be pointless to attempt any list. Virtually any software of interest will run under MS-DOS if it runs on a PC at all.

In a company with any significant number of PCs, the main problems are likely to be not availability but choosing the software that best fits the requirements and then restricting users to the packages chosen. Paradoxically in a discussion of availability, failure to restrict choice in this instance can lead to severe problems of support and training if too many different solutions to the same problem are allowed.

Fortunately, a number of magazines regularly publish software reviews and also indexes of the reviews in previous issues. These form a good basis for making an initial shortlist of software that may meet requirements. Among the more respected magazines are *Byte*, *Personal Computer World* and *PC User*. These are available in most newsagents and bookshops for £2–3. There is also a large directory of MS-DOS/PC-DOS software produced by VNU in the *PC Users' Year Book* (£95 from VNU, 32–34 Broadwick Street, London W1A 2HG).

The newer, growing market for the second wave of more powerful PCs, based on the Intel 386 and 486 chips, is characterised by two environments: OS/2 and UNIX. It should be understood that MS-DOS software will run on these machines as well; a typical configuration of a PC based on these chips will support the more sophisticated facilities offered by OS/2 and UNIX.

The OS/2 environment is proprietary to IBM; it is "open" in the

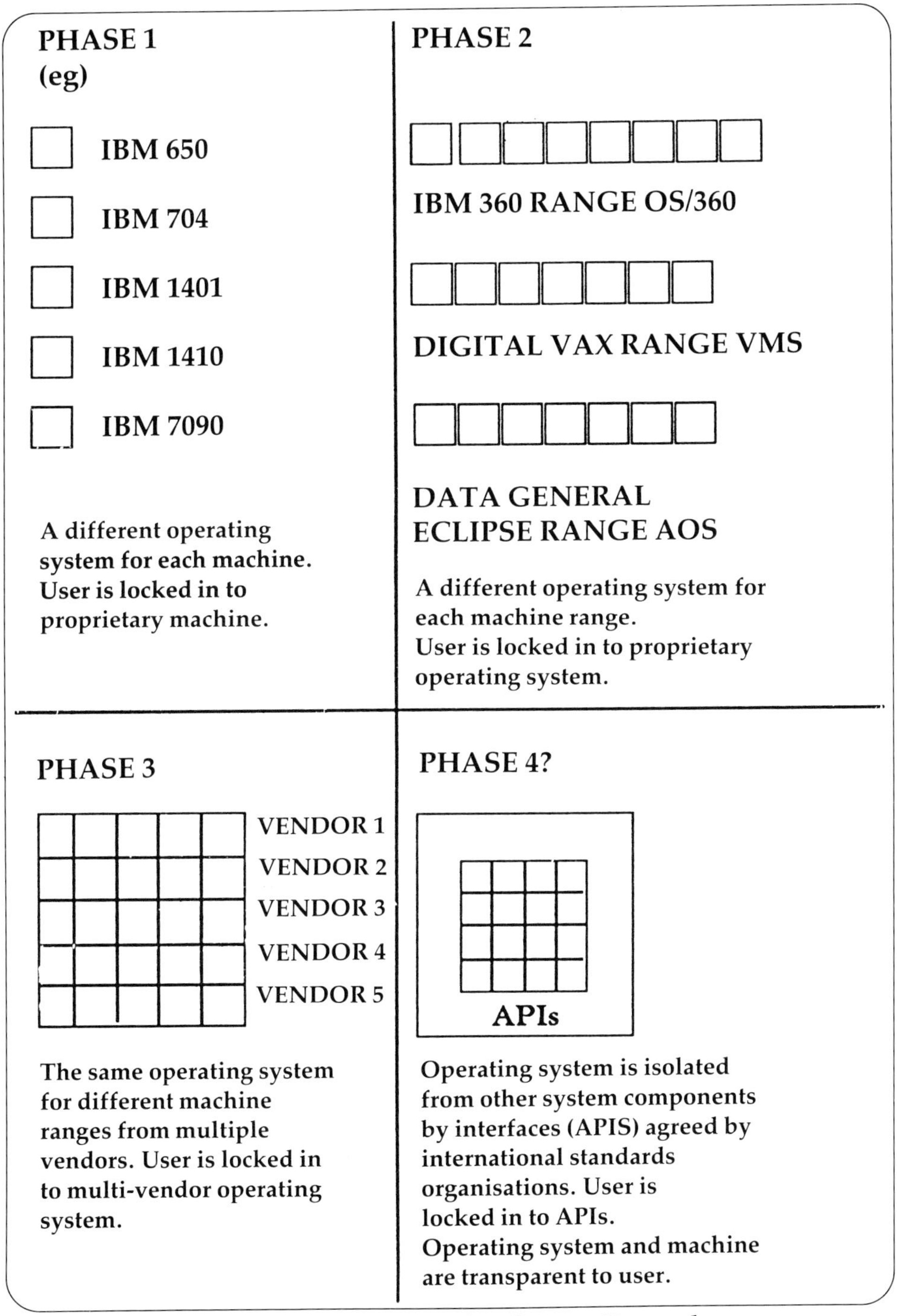

PHASE 1
(eg)

☐ **IBM 650**

☐ **IBM 704**

☐ **IBM 1401**

☐ **IBM 1410**

☐ **IBM 7090**

A different operating
system for each machine.
User is locked in to
proprietary machine.

PHASE 2

IBM 360 RANGE OS/360

DIGITAL VAX RANGE VMS

**DATA GENERAL
ECLIPSE RANGE AOS**

A different operating system for
each machine range.
User is locked in to proprietary
operating system.

PHASE 3

VENDOR 1
VENDOR 2
VENDOR 3
VENDOR 4
VENDOR 5

The same operating system
for different machine
ranges from multiple
vendors. User is locked in
to multi-vendor operating
system.

PHASE 4?

APIs

Operating system is isolated
from other system components
by interfaces (APIS) agreed by
international standards
organisations. User is
locked in to APIs.
Operating system and machine
are transparent to user.

Figure 9.1   Phases In Operating System Dependency

limited sense that PC-DOS is open, but without there being any equivalent to MS-DOS to allow a wider market. OS/2 is certainly not a derivative of UNIX. OS/2 already has a sufficiently large market base for it to be an important environment, although whether it achieves the importance of the MS-DOS/PC-DOS environment depends on its success relative to that of UNIX. For the moment, the outcome is far from certain.

The best source of information on software to run under OS/2 is IBM itself; simply call the nearest IBM sales office or your local IBM agent. The availability of software to run under UNIX is dealt with below.

Workstations

The term "workstation" has been used generally to describe the very powerful type of PC that is used, for instance, in computer-aided design (CAD) or for scientific work. The term is now used more generally to describe any PC with the power to support several applications running at one time. PCs of the near future are expected to be genuinely multi-purpose, handling electronic mail, image processing and other standard office functions that are currently considered slightly exotic. The CAD/scientific workstations have typically used UNIX as an operating system, and so UNIX has built up a lead in terms of market base in this area.

In the commercial environment, the availability of engineering workstation functionality at the price of a high-end PC will ensure that UNIX workstations will have a role on the desktop of the business professional.

MID-RANGE MULTI-USER ENVIRONMENTS

There is only one open environment in this arena, and that is UNIX. The two significantly large proprietary environments are delimited by the IBM OS/400 operating system and the Digital VMS operating system. Both of these have stimulated quite extensive numbers of third-party suppliers to emerge, and both offer or promise a degree of portability. In IBM's case, the portability is to be provided through its Systems Application Architecture (SAA). In Digital's case, the portability is via the span covered by its VMS operating system, which runs in different but upwardly compatible versions on machines from workstation size to mainframe size. In both of these cases, details of software availability are best obtained via the environment owners, IBM and Digital.

The UNIX arena is currently larger than either of the main proprietary environments mentioned, and is growing faster. The problem of constraining users to one solution per problem, mentioned above in the context of MS-DOS, is not likely to occur frequently, since we are talking about multi-user systems. However, there is the problem of choice from among the many potentially relevant packages, and there is no generally available set of respected reviews such as is available through magazines in the MS-DOS environment. So evaluation has to be done by each installation. See Figure 9.1.

Core software

At the heart of any installation today will be a set of software that forms the foundation for all applications to be run. We will call this *core software*. It includes the operating system, obviously, which will be UNIX in the case of open systems, and also some system utilities. Perhaps most importantly of all, it will include database software to hold the corporate data and a set of associated development tools.

The generally accepted model for database management systems (DBMSs) in the mid-range arena is the relational model originally proposed by Ted Codd. The major suppliers of relational DBMSs and the major suppliers of associated development tools, generically known as computer-aided software engineering (CASE) tools, were at one time in danger of overlapping arbitrarily into one another's markets. There was a danger that the main players such as Oracle, Information Builders, Relational Technology, Informix, etc would each provide products that were strong in one half of the picture but relatively weak in the other. Since the DBMS used is intimately tied to most applications, the danger was that users would escape (to UNIX) from operating-system dependencies only to find themselves locked into DBMS dependencies. The danger persists in some proprietary environments, but has been averted in the case of open systems by a general agreement between the relevant suppliers on the framework that will apply to this area.

Broadly, what is proposed is that, rather than there being a struggle for a single standard DBMS and a single standard set of CASE tools, there should be a standard linkage between the two. The linkage will be standard SQL. Users will thus be able to mix and match CASE tools and DBMSs, provided that all communicate via standard SQL. All of the major DBMS and CASE-tool vendors now subscribe to this philosophy, and together provide a much richer development environment than is available from any proprietary environment in the mid-range arena.

Of the other major components of core software, system utilities have been a weak point, but one that is fast being corrected; instrumentation for monitoring resource usage and system performance remains a problem for the moment.

Office systems can perhaps also be regarded nowadays as core software; although they are really an application, the software is pervasive, and intrinsic to all business functions. Office systems have been at the leading edge of open systems, and constitute their earliest success story. Even companies that do not yet count UNIX as a strategic environment frequently run their office systems under UNIX, simply because the richest functionality, the widest choice and the greatest cost-effectiveness is available under UNIX. In this respect office systems could provide the paradigm for the open systems market generally.

Sources of mid-range software

Finding out exactly what is available is not too difficult. Your first port of call should be any prospective supplier. All suppliers of any significance supply some version of UNIX in addition to any proprietary environment. All of them also keep lists of software available to run under their chosen version of UNIX. Simply ask each supplier for their list. Some care may need to be taken in "mixing and matching" applications from different suppliers, although there should be few problems with mainstream UNIX suppliers. There may be more difficulty with software from suppliers whose principal focus is not UNIX but a proprietary environment, and whose business strategy does not depend on the success of open systems. The preceding chapter on UNIX should clarify this point.

A more comprehensive view of software that runs under UNIX is given by the *Catalog of UNIX System V Software* published by AT&T. This lists hundreds of applications broken down into, for instance, DBMSs, general business applications (such as accounts), spreadsheets, graphics, integrated general tools, software development tools and numerous vertical sectors defined by their SIC (Standard Industrial Classification) codes. The fact that it runs to close to 2000 pages and has 9 pages of trademark acknowledgements should give some idea of its scope. This should be at least one version of the UNIX user's bible. The catalogue is obtainable through any AT&T office and is published by Simon Schuster (Prentice-Hall).

A further directory of interest is the *Software Users' Year Book* published by VNU. Unfortunately this does not separate UNIX software from other, proprietary, software available. However, there are separate categories for such items as DBMSs, system utilities, applications programs by vertical sector and various other types of software, and operating-system dependency is noted for each program. It is available from VNU, 32–34 Broadwick Street, London WlA 2HG, price £95.

MAINFRAME ENVIRONMENTS

There is only one environment relevant to very large general-purpose computers that has received very wide acceptance and acquired a large third-party market, and that is proprietary. It is the IBM MVS environment. So far there is no version of UNIX that can support the very high throughput of mixed workloads that MVS systems typically handle. The applicable architecture is SAA, which has a limited degree of openness; details of software that conform to it can best be obtained directly from IBM.

There is some discussion as to the future of the traditional mainframe environment. Statements that "the mainframe is dead" have been common for some 15 years now, and are still premature. What is certain is that large mainframes have been evolving towards being essentially database machines. Also, the old single central processor has become a complex of up to six tightly coupled processors. The technology and economics of data processing seem to be driving towards complexes that include both loosely and tightly coupled processors in what is generally termed a distributed systems environment. How long that evolution will take is uncertain.

In these circumstances, it is unknown whether UNIX will ever need to evolve to include the facilities typical of a mainframe operating system. For the moment, all such environments are proprietary, and IBM's MVS is the leading one.

NETWORKING ENVIRONMENTS

The environments most relevant to networking software are OSI, TCP/IP and SNA. The first two are truly open, the last is proprietary to IBM. Of the first two, TCP/IP is diminishing in significance as OSI becomes more complete.

SNA (Systems Network Architecture) is the environment that has so far achieved greatest acceptance in the commercial marketplace. It was the first of the three to be defined, and has more products that implement it than either of the others. Most suppliers provide links into it in one form or another from their own proprietary systems, but SNA itself, and any information on software that implements it, belongs essentially to IBM.

TCP/IP was a US Department of Defense initiative that had the merit of being implemented more quickly than the corresponding elements of OSI. It is an open environment for all practical purposes, and has been used in some cases as an OSI substitute until OSI catches up. Its significance now is less than it has been, and will diminish further in the future.

OSI has suffered in the past from the slowness of standards bodies generally in reaching agreed definitions, and also from an initial reluctance on the part of many suppliers to provide products that met the standards. However, OSI received strong backing from European and US governments unwilling to be tied to proprietary environments, and those early handicaps are now disappearing. Many companies with international networks based necessarily on SNA have developed a policy of switching to OSI as and when feasible.

Perhaps the major reference on OSI software is a directory produced by the Department of Trade and Industry (DTI) and called simply *OSI Products*. The body of the book, after some 90 pages of general information, consists of a description of the relevant products and plans for 25 major suppliers, including all the major players in the computer industry. It is available from the DTI IT Standards Unit, Kingsgate House, 66–74 Victoria Street, London SW1E 6SW.

While OSI is emerging as the route to networking standards, it is worth mentioning an important de facto standard for the integration of PC and server networks. This is Novell's NetWare System, which is portable across a wide range of operating environments, and which, according to some surveys, accounts for up to 70% of installed PC/server local area networks.

10 Advances in hardware

It will be news to no one that advances in computer hardware are continuous and provide the potential for ever-improved cost performance. The generally accepted norm is a gain of around 20% per year. However, some recent developments have made much greater gains possible, either directly or indirectly, and all are associated with open systems. They are the advent of commodity chip sets, a focus on scalability and the emergence of RISC architectures.

COMMODITY CHIP SETS

Commodity chip sets are chip sets that have achieved mass usage through their use in PCs and can thus be regarded as commodities in the building of CPUs; they are commented on in various contexts elsewhere in this book.

Their importance lies primarily in their relative cheapness, since they can be mass-produced, and in their impact on the portability of software. An instruction set that is common between different machines and is available in machines covering a reasonably wide range of power is only one factor in portability and compatibility, but it is a fundamentally important one.

Perhaps the most obvious examples of chip sets that qualify for the adjective "commodity" are the Intel 80XXX and Motorola 68XXX chip sets.

SCALABILITY

The term "scalability" is generally used to mean fine granularity in differences in power between CPUs within a given range.

When a supplier designs a range of processors, a potential power band for all processors within the range is defined. The normal design objective is that all machines within the range should be upwardly compatible with respect to hardware and operating-system architecture. This means that, as far as the user is concerned, applications always run on larger configurations in the same way that they run on smaller ones. However, that does not mean that the underlying hardware and system software are implemented in exactly the same way on all configurations; they simply carry out the same functions that the user sees.

In fact, there are good technical reasons why large machines should be implemented differently from small machines. A supplier will therefore have several machine designs in mind (all conforming to the same architecture) when a new range of machines is planned. There may, for instance, be four separate processor designs within a range.

Simply supplying four CPUs over a power band that could provide a power ratio of 50:1 (or even much more) provides very poor granularity. A user whose needs just exceeded the power of one processor would be forced into an upgrade involving a great deal more power and a corresponding price tag. Suppliers therefore create various "models" of each separate processor design with the aim of providing better granularity. A CPU may be "slugged" (underexploited) or have some artificial constraint placed on it, such as only allowing a certain amount of memory or disk to be supplied with it, in order to create smaller models. Incorporation of faster technology may be used similarly to create larger models. The overall result may be a dozen or so CPUs within the range, greatly improving the granularity (scalability).

Virtually all computer ranges are planned in this way. The relevance of open systems lies in the possibility of acquiring compatible CPUs from different vendors. Since suppliers choose different power bands and subdivide them between CPUs in different ways, there is an inevitable overlap between CPUs from different suppliers over any given power band. This overlap provides much better scalability over a range of open systems than is likely to be available from any single vendor. Users can therefore match machines much more exactly to their require-ments, and do not have to carry excess machine power unnecessarily or resort to fine tuning of their systems to stave off an upgrade.

THE SIGNIFICANCE OF RISC

The acronym RISC (Reduced Instruction Set Computer) is used as a contrast to CISC (Complex Instruction Set Computer), and, to appreciate the distinction, it is useful to understand a little about the development of computer instruction sets.

All computers were, and still are, based fundamentally on Boolean logic, on the well-known logical AND, OR and NOT functions. These very simple functions are used in combination to make up less primitive functions that we all easily recognise, eg add, multiply, divide, etc. These and other similar ones are all basic functions within a computer.

Implementing these functions, collectively known as the computer's instruction set, in hardware circuitry constitutes a major part of the cost of building a computer. For this reason it has been common in the past for some cheaper machines to have only a very small set of basic instructions, not even including divide, for instance. The more complex instructions had to be available, but were implemented by calls to software routines, which used combinations of the basic instructions. Later, microcode tended to be used rather than software. In either case, the objective was to reduce the cost of building the machine. The penalty was that the more complex instructions executed relatively slowly.

As the cost of technology fell and more computers were being sold, so it became cost-justifiable to implement more and more instructions directly in hardware circuitry. Nowadays, functions that in early machines would have always been implemented as software routines are implemented routinely in hardware. One consequence is that the size of instruction sets has grown. A 1960s computer might have only around 100 instructions implemented in hardware; a modern one may have over 300. Computers that have these large instruction sets are known as CISC machines.

Why have large instruction sets?

One reason for large (complex) instruction sets is that the instruction set as a whole executes faster, providing more "bangs per buck". Another is that there is a saving in the use of memory; using one instruction to carry out a function rather than many means fewer instructions per program and hence less memory required to store the program.

Two recent factors have altered this line of reasoning. Firstly, the cost of fabricating memory (whatever you actually pay for it) has fallen dramatically; this negates one of the arguments above.

The second factor is more complicated. One aspect of it is the apparent universal truth of the 80-20 principle. Measurements of how frequently particular instructions are used have shown that only a small part of an instruction set is used very frequently and these instructions tend to be the simple ones. These instructions therefore have a disproportionate effect on the overall speed of the machine in practice. If they are engineered to execute very fast, other instructions can execute much more slowly without having a significant impact on overall machine performance.

The other aspect is that the economics of semiconductor techno-logy have reached the point where simple instruction sets can be implemented very cheaply on a single chip. This is partly due to the technology itself, and partly due to the fact that a simple instruction set has very wide generality and so can be sold in large volumes for use on many different machines. The combination of these factors means a quantum drop in the cost of building machines with simple instruction sets without any significant loss in performance. This is the origin of the term RISC machines, but the term now means more.

Other elements of RISC

The engineering of the instruction set is only one factor, albeit an important one, in the overall performance of a machine. It is generally agreed that further performance gains in CISC machines are becoming very difficult to realise; the technology is reaching the limits of its potential. RISC machines, on the other hand, provide a new approach and a large cost advantage as "working capital", allowing machine designers to look for other ways to extract greater performance from the machines they are designing.

Understanding all the possibilities for extracting increased per-formance would entail a course in computer engineering. Suffice it to say here that memory caches, pipelining, embedded controllers and a variety of other technical "tricks" are all part and parcel of the RISC concept.

In point of fact, most of the concepts behind RISC architectures came not from hardware designers but from software developers working on advanced compilers optimised for implementing portable languages such as C. Therein lies the key. The simple chip sets that were fundamental to the PC revolution, and which are now generally known as commodity chip sets, when used in conjunction with easily portable operating systems and languages, provide the technical basis for open systems. RISC architectures are about exploiting these commodity chip sets to gain the maximum performance within the general constraint of what commodity chip sets can provide. Those constraints are currently unknown since their boundaries have not yet been encountered. What *is* known, however, is that a lot of untapped potential remains and that an open-systems environment will encourage innovators to innovate.

SUMMARY

The above developments in computer hardware offer users the potential for much larger gains in the price performance of their equipment than the traditional "industry standard" of 20% per year. Most advances in technology and in the way that computers are built apply as much to proprietary systems as they do to open ones. However, in a proprietary market there may be little incentive for a supplier to pass on the full cost benefits made possible by advances in hardware to users who are locked in. In an open market-place, competition should ensure that users derive the maximum advantage.

11 Object orientation

GENERAL CONCEPTS

If object orientation is explained to lay people, their most common reaction is to wonder why any other approach was ever used. The answer to that question lies in the origin of computers; so that, briefly, is where we will start.

The earliest computers were built as special-purpose machines for dealing with specific scientific problems. Even when it was realised that computers were capable of very general application, that generality was at first confined primarily to scientific and engineering problems. The earliest languages (eg Algol, Fortran) generally resembled mathematical notations, and the data structures catered for were typically arrays, matrices, etc. The first implementations of UNIX, incidentally, although coming much later, did not allow for record handling.

From the mid-1960s onwards, as computers came to be used more generally for commercial applications, so languages were developed to incorporate ordinary English words (eg Move, Find, Open, Close), and the structures catered for were typically records and files as in any form of business system.

From about 1980, text applications started to appear in large numbers, requiring new structures to be catered for: pages and documents (these are in fact sometimes called unstructured files). More recently, image processing has emerged as a major new application area, sound is being processed for speech recognition and synthesis systems, and (just as importantly) increasing numbers of applications call for the hybridisation of these various application "types" and their corresponding structures (or "unstructures").

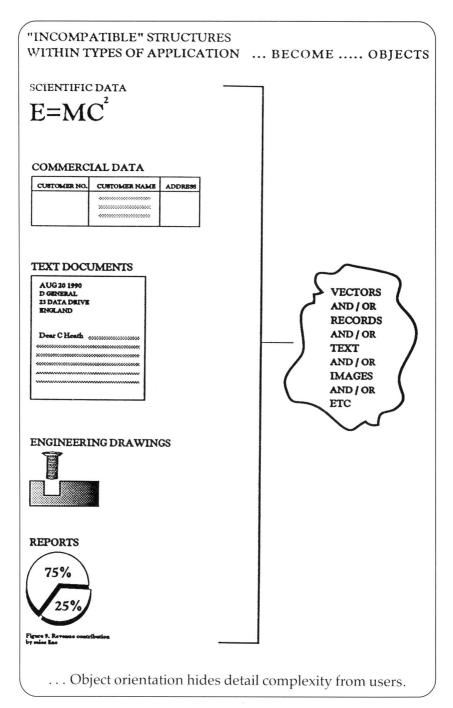

Figure 11.1   Example of Object Orientation

The result is that it is no longer appropriate to think of the IT world, or of any significant part of it, as consisting of any of the traditional single structures. However, we do need a way of thinking about *things* before we get into the detail of exactly how we will store and process them. This way is *object orientation*; the *things* are objects.

In a sense that brings our thinking full circle. Early systems had a very technical user interface, and the relatively high cost of the technology forced problems to be presented to the machine in a very detailed form for reasons of efficiency.

Those factors corrupted our normal way of thinking, which is to think about objects. The sophistication and economics of modern technology allow us to revert to our normal style of thinking.

WHAT IS AN OBJECT?

So what is an object in computer terms? Essentially, an object can be anything you like—anything that you care to isolate as a separate item in your thinking about a particular problem or application. It is simply a higher-order abstraction than any of the items mentioned above (records, documents, images, arrays). In practice, because the ultimate purpose is to produce a representation of an application that we can process, we impose some order on the objects we select by grouping them in classes. The class any given object belongs to depends on the significant characteristics, for given purposes, that it shares with other objects. Classes can be broken down into sub-classes, sub-classes into sub-sub-classes, etc.

Since any object will normally be processed, one set of its characteristics that must be significant is whether it is in fact a file or data record, a text string, an image, an array, etc, or some combination of these. That information affects how it can be processed, and at that level of detail we are back to the more traditional view of computing. What we have done through object orientation is simply to hide the traditional level of detail and to allow ourselves a more natural view of the problems/applications we wish to think about. This is demonstrated in Figure 11.1.

That is not quite the end of the story, because there are implications for the way that software works in our new object-oriented world, and also for what we see on computer screens. Since objects are a higher-order (less detailed) abstraction, they are intrinsically more portable; they contain less detail about how they are to be processed—detail that could link them directly to a specific machine architecture.

The converse of being more portable is that objects require more translation before they can be processed on any specific machine. The extra translation implies more (machine) resources and hence more cost (see Chapter 6: *Compatibility and portability*). So it is likely that object-oriented architectures will be implemented first where there is a clear pay-off (CAD/CAM is one obvious application) and gradually introduced more generally, sometimes initially in a somewhat bastardised form. This is already happening to some extent in database systems, where entity-relationship DBMSs contain some of the attributes of object-oriented architectures.

Some languages were mentioned above in connection with certain data structures. Objects also require different kinds of language, of which the most notable today is C++. Object-oriented languages owe their origin to modelling languages, of which Simula was an early and respected example. The portability of object-oriented programs derives in part from a specific characteristic of object-oriented languages: that any function must apply consistently to all objects, whatever their nature. Technically, that is known as polymorphism.

Further portability is derived from the ability to store code with data as a single object, which allows specialised co-processors and distributed architectures to be exploited more easily in configurations where these exist. Technically, this is known as encapsulation.

All aspects of object orientation in fact recognise explicitly what software developers have failed to recognise generally at great cost: namely, that all computing is modelling—creating a representation of some aspect of reality for some purpose at some point in time. Modelling is not just a specialisation within computing. The understanding that that perception provides explains many of the ills that have bedevilled software development. Object orientation holds the potential to remove them eventually at a generally acceptable level of cost-efficiency.

The most immediate and obvious evidence of the move towards object orientation is to be found on many computer screens: icons. Icons represent objects, and graphical user interfaces (GUIs) based around icons are set to become the standard for the industry.

GRAPHICAL USER INTERFACES

The general objective of graphical user interfaces (GUIs) is to provide all users of all applications with a single, simple set of conventions for accessing and working with applications. There are several such graphical user interfaces currently contending to be the standard, among them OSF/Motif, X-Windows, Presentation Manager, MS-Windows, New Wave and OpenLook.

Industry watchers have fun discussing the relative merits of each, and predicting the likely eventual "winner", much in the same way as they discussed the many "flavours" of UNIX two or three years ago. A new GUI, Windows 3 from Microsoft, for example, has recently been announced and promises to be very influential. For the moment, the differences between these GUIs is a problem mainly for software developers, who must choose to design their applications to one, or to a small subset, of those available. X-Windows is probably the most widely used GUI currently, and is becoming the subject of standardisation effort. Presentation Manager, on the other hand, is the IBM proprietary standard, and OSF/Motif (Figure 11.2) is the OSF standard, also looked on with favour by UNIX International.

It is not the differences, however, but the similarities that concern us here. It seems certain that over the next couple of years the number of significant differences between GUIs will diminish, and so will the number of effective contenders. Also, tools to port GUIs between applications, which are already around, will increase and improve. For all these reasons, we can be confident of increasing standardisation of the user interface, and eventually a standard "look and feel".

The components of a GUI

The general "look and feel" of the new GUIs will be familiar to anybody who has seen or used an Apple Macintosh. Apple has done pioneering work in this field, and in a sense has set the

Figure 11.2   OSF/Motif

standard. The company does not appear, however, to be greatly involved with standardisation efforts.

All the principal GUIs provide a hierarchical directory displayed in the form of icons. All provide a set of conventions for moving through the directory, for opening a window on an application and for other basic accessing functions such as browsing, editing, saving, etc. They also enable the user to have access to multiple applications simultaneously and to pass objects between them. In this last respect they incorporate elements of multi-tasking operating systems (Figure 11.3).

There are many possible differences in the way these facilities are programmed. We will not go into these differences here, but they are the substance of any differences between GUIs. It should be apparent, even from the brief description above, that GUIs consist of much more than simply icons on screens. Many of the important benefits, however, do not rely on detailed standardisation.

As indicated earlier, GUIs are a natural part of object-oriented

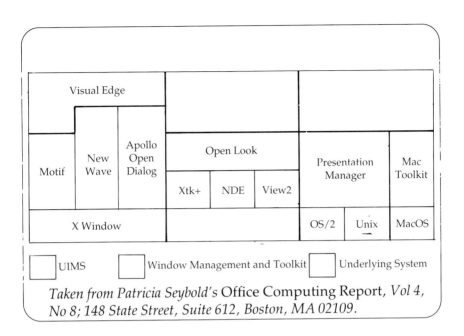

Figure 11.3   GUI Capabilities: Products Mapped to Three Layers

systems. They also fit naturally with distributed network computing, since they should allow a user to open a window on an application wherever it resides physically in a network (although Presentation Manager doesn't at the time of writing). They also conform to the client-server architecture, although in X-Windows, for instance, the server (GUI) is on the PC and the client (application) possibly on a larger machine (see *Client-server architectures* in the next chapter).

All of these factors contribute to ease of use, but it is the simplicity and consistency of the means used to carry out tasks that are most important to users. To this extent, differences in icons, for instance, are less important than differences in the conventions used to manipulate them, and it is on this area that standardisation efforts are likely to focus initially.

The promise of GUIs is to provide an interface that is consistent and easy to learn and use, whether for local or for remote applications, and that conforms to the new kinds of architecture being introduced to IT systems. The promise has yet to be fulfilled, but the foundations are mostly laid and progress is rapid.

STANDARDISATION OF OBJECT-ORIENTED SYSTEMS

Although object-oriented systems are relatively new in the commercial field, work on implementing aspects of them has been going on for a decade, and the principal design ideas go back over more than 20 years. Still, commercial implementations are new, and there is the opportunity for standards to be created before too much investment in ad hoc implementations has to be taken into account.

A broad alliance of suppliers has come together to form the Object Management Group (OMG), based in Framingham, Massachusetts. This is not a standards body in the sense that ISO is, and does not seek to define the "best possible" standards. It is perhaps best described in its own terms:

> "The end purpose is to define a living standard with realised (not realisable, but realised) parts, so that applications developers can deliver their applications with off-the-shelf components for common facilities like object storage, class structure, peripheral interface, user interface, etc. ... the OMG presents a book of interface specifications for which modules may be had— immediately, for many hardware platforms, in a large domain of operating systems, and in a large set of languages. Furthermore, the portions of the standard are interoperable with each other and portable to many different platforms."

OMG has defined a reference model which, though incomplete, is being extended and used to guide the setting of standards. In our explanation of object orientation, we have not used the OMG definition of an object, but feel that it should be included for those with a specific technical interest. It reads:

> "An object is a combination of an associated state and a set of operations which explicitly embodies an abstraction characterised by the behaviour of relevant requests."

12 The new applications environment

Over the last two years or so, some clear signs of order have been imposed on the previous chaos that reigned in the world of applications. This applies not only to the environment in which applications run but also to the environment in which they are developed. There are now models for both and progress is being made in implementing the key structures.

As a basis for understanding what is, and what will be, let us briefly look first at what has been.

WHAT'S IN AN APPLICATION?

Twenty-five years or more ago, virtually all the code necessary to run an application had to be written into the application program itself. This would even include, for instance, the 250 or so instructions required to open a magnetic tape file. System utilities were generally only just starting to appear, and the operating system consisted of little more than a bootstrap routine and some elementary system-control functions.

What then happened, in effect, was that software developers realised they were having to code the same functions over and over again for different applications. It would clearly be more efficient if functions that were common to many programs could be coded once and made available from a central library of some sort. Routines to open and close files were among the first to be "got out of the way". Other file-handling routines and report-generation facilities quickly followed, relieving programmers of many of these repetitious (and error-prone) tasks.

As the state of the art progressed, many more facilities were added to the operating system, and libraries of utilities appeared, as did such useful basic tools as DBMSs, TP monitors, etc.

A further dimension was added as interactive use of computers gained ground, particularly when PCs appeared, in that a lot of effort had to be directed at creating the user interface. Screen painters, tool boxes and widget libraries started to appear for the same reasons as the earlier utility libraries had been created.

The result of all this is that very little of the code that is used in an application is, as it were, "hand-written"; very little of the code executed is written for the application itself. By far the largest part is either generated via tools executed from library routines called by the program, or consists of operating-system services.

So the answer to our question "What's in an application?" is "Very little code that is specific to the application". That is important as a basis for understanding the strengths and weaknesses of the current situation and the direction that applications are taking.

APPLICATION PROGRAMMING INTERFACES

The provision of central code libraries and extended operating services has done much to improve the efficiency of program-ming. However, in nearly all cases, these central libraries are tied to specific (proprietary) operating systems or major system-software components such as a DBMS or a TP monitor. The set of central routines (or services) associated with any operating system, DBMS, etc may provide essentially similar functions, but each will do so in its own way. The same function, for instance, may be provided by a different module in different operating systems, may be called in a different way, and in general may provide the programmer with a different interface.

As a result, application programs calling these routines are locked into the system software that provides them. The key to opening up the applications environment is to find a means of reducing and eventually eliminating an application program's dependency on the utility libraries and system-software services that it uses. This means is generically known as an *application programming interface* (API).

Essentially, an application programming interface (API) defines where, in relation to any set of central services, the application-

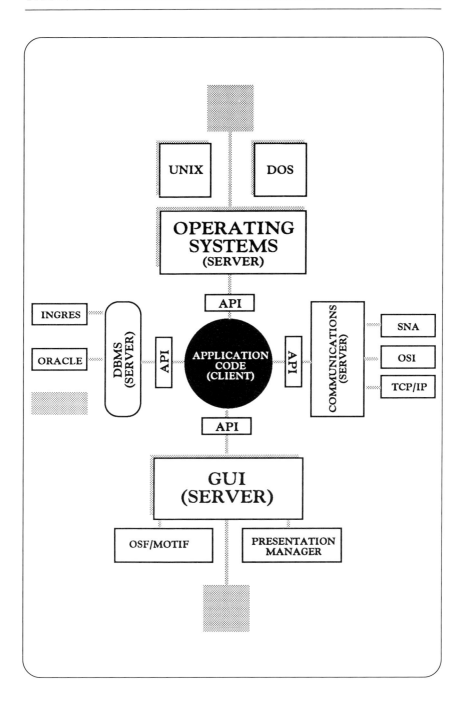

Figure 12.1   The (Simplified) Shape of Future Applications

intrinsic code ends and the service code starts. It further defines which set of services belongs where, and how the programmer should be able to call them. So far, few APIs have been developed, although many are in the process of being defined. What is important for now is that it is becoming quite clear where APIs should be located, and in general terms what they should consist of.

The future application

Although it is not yet possible to isolate application-specific code from generally applicable routines, that desirable state is already on the horizon. There is in fact quite a large number of APIs that could be relevant to programs and systems as a whole, but we will simplify that to illustrate the direction in which application programming is headed (Figure 12.1).

The principal functions likely to be required by most commercial applications, and that can and should be provided centrally rather than written or generated for each application, have to do with the user interface, the operating system, file handling and communications. We can therefore envisage a time when the programmer will be provided with an API for each of these four sets of services. The programmer writes only the code that is specific to the application, and includes within it standard calls to any service required as defined by the APIs. Clearly, this will increase even further the efficiency with which programmers can work. Also, and most importantly, the existence of APIs will greatly increase the portability of the application programs. All that should need to be ported is the application-specific code, and the APIs will take care of differences in system software.

CLIENT-SERVER ARCHITECTURES

Client-server architectures have received a lot of media attention over the last year, and seem capable of various interpretations. So we had better make clear what we understand by them.

In fact, their essence is already explained by the model of future applications described above. The client in a client-server architecture is the application (or user); the server is the mechanism that provides the services that applications need to supplement the application-specific code. The concept derives from the theory of large, shared file-stores.

In common parlance, PCs are often referred to as clients, while larger machines are referred to as servers. This is really only an extension of our definition of client-server architectures, in that it is generally expected that the applications will increasingly run on PCs while file-handling, communications services, etc will typically be provided on larger machines.

It is important to note, however, that the client-server architecture is essentially a software architecture; it provides a dichotomy between application-specific code and general system services. That dichotomy remains valid whatever hardware is used to run the application, and is not dependent on whether expectations prove to be true, with respect to PCs or any other machines.

A weakness in client-server architectures is that there is as yet no general definition of what should be regarded as client code and what as server code. However, the distinction is broadly, intuitively clear and will become clearer as more APIs are defined.

That weakness is more than offset by the strengths of the client-server model. Applications change over time in broadly two ways: changes to the logic of the application, resulting from changes to the requirements originally specified; and changes in the volume of the workload being processed. The client-server model has the potential to isolate the former in the client code and the latter in the server. Changes in volume (upwards) should normally be satisfied by running the server code on a larger system.

There are other strengths to the client-server model that appear in distributed systems. In a network of distributed systems, the model makes it easier to isolate or group services, as required, flexibly onto different configurations of machines. That in turn makes it easier to optimise the use of the current configuration and make small incremental changes to the configuration as the overall workload grows, rather than having to face expensive upgrades as thresholds are reached.

Similar points are true of the client code. The model makes it easier to implement applications incrementally, as the code size grows to exceed thresholds, or as extra modules of application code are required.

THE DEVELOPMENT ENVIRONMENT

The development environment itself is changing in response to requirements for a more standard approach to application development. As was pointed out elsewhere in this book, CASE tools have frequently failed to deliver on their promises because of the lack of a general model of a development environment into which they should fit.

A focus on this issue in recent years has resulted in IBM announcing its AD/Cycle, and in international standards organisations working on projects such as the Information Resource Dictionary System (IRDS) and the Portable Common Tools Environment (PCTE).

The core of such models is a repository, or directory, in which all development work is referenced. Although this is in essence a type of conventional data dictionary, running on a conventional database system, it really needs to be object-oriented, since it must contain documentation and diagrams as well as code and data. There also needs to be a standard interface between the tools and the repository, allowing many different types of tool to access and manipulate elements of the application under development. And finally, there needs to be a common means of accessing the various tools.

However, there are some other essential elements on which agreement seems less clear. Project-management aspects of the model appear in AD/Cycle as a separate module, whereas they may more properly be regarded as a separate dimension. Instrumentation, which should also be a separate dimension, seems so far to be largely ignored.

Nonetheless, a clearer picture of the development environment of the future is coming together, and some of the core elements are available now.

13 Choosing a supplier

A PROBLEM LIKE THAT OF THE RENAISSANCE

Paradoxically, whilst freedom of choice is one of the great benefits of open systems, it also poses problems of its own. In a market made up primarily of standard components, subsystems built from commodity chip sets, etc, how can the complexity of choices offered be simplified and reduced to manageable proportions?

Just as in the feudal societies of the Middle Ages the barons created simple, secure lives for their serfs, relieving them of all important decisions, so proprietary environments have accustomed most users to manoeuvring within a narrow choice-band. Although very restrictive, this simplifies decision-making, sometimes to the point of deciding on the least unacceptable solution. Erich Fromm in his seminal work *Fear of Freedom* points out that although serfs were free *to* do very little they were also free *from* most of life's hard decisions.

Open systems, by contrast, represent the Renaissance. They free users from the shackles of proprietary environments, but force them to deal effectively with their greater freedom of choice. So the problem we address here is how to isolate the important factors from the less relevant detail, and thereby simplify the decision process.

LISTS OF PREFERRED SUPPLIERS

It is customary for large corporate IT departments to operate lists of preferred suppliers, even for proprietary environments. This has the effect of pre-qualifying potential suppliers, and where formal substantiation of purchasing decisions is required, it can reduce or eliminate the need for invitations to tender.

For preferred suppliers lists to be useful, they must contain some optimal number of sources. A hundred suppliers in a list is clearly as useless as only one. For any one category such as processors, large disks, LANs, etc, a list of six potential sources is likely to be an upper limit; just two or three may serve all practical purposes, and three or four may be the usual case.

The precise number will depend on how total IT requirements are broken down, and on the criteria pertaining at any individual company. Bear in mind that the objective is to simplify decision-making without making the process arbitrary. Typically, such lists will not include all the suppliers that meet the criteria employed, but rather will limit themselves to those suppliers that meet the criteria best.

With proprietary environments, the main problem may be to find more than one or two suppliers who meet the minimal criteria. With open systems, the problem is more likely to be one of extending and tightening the necessary criteria (relevantly) in order to restrict contending suppliers to a manageable number.

Whatever the case, it will be important to ensure that preferred suppliers lists are of a manageable size. Lists that are too extensive defeat the object of having them, and will entail unnecessary expense in the decision-making process.

The major criteria likely to be relevant in the general case are discussed below, in a sequence running broadly from the more general to the more particular. These criteria are generally the same as those used in Appendix 2, where Data General has provided a checklist of questions to put to open-systems suppliers.

COMMITMENT TO OPEN SYSTEMS

A major but intangible criterion is the degree of commitment of any given vendor to the open-systems market. At an open-systems event in particular, it will be difficult to find any supplier who does not claim to be totally committed to open systems; moreover, it will be equally difficult on the spot to prove otherwise.

Some of the questions suggested in Appendix 2 will help to differentiate between suppliers, but this is an area that will need some further homework. Most of the major suppliers have been in existence for some time, and are responsible for proprietary environments as well as being involved in open ones; they are necessarily committed to maintaining the former as well as exploiting the latter. The questions to be asked must therefore be helpful in assessing to what extent a supplier is committed to open systems.

One way of approaching this problem is to ask about representation on standards bodies. Suppliers genuinely committed to open systems will be represented, for instance, on alternative bodies as well as on the general spectrum of bodies covering different aspects of IT. Membership of alternative bodies can be regarded cynically as hedging one's bets; on the other hand, it can be seen as a commitment to open standards generally, no matter which standard eventually achieves general acceptance.

Interconnection to widely used proprietary environments—SNA, for instance—is also a sign of commitment to practical open systems. It is worth finding out what proprietary protocols the supplier can emulate, not just when he is asked but as a part of the standard product portfolio.

Finally, it may be interesting to find out where the current R&D budget is going. Currently, most suppliers will be devoting most of their R&D budget to proprietary systems, both as a matter of necessity and as a result of previous plans. R&D is intrinsically a long-term activity, and budgets for it cannot be switched at a moment's notice. However, if the supplier is serious about open systems, there should already be a discernible, growing emphasis on open systems at the expense of proprietary ones. Differences over the last two years, and commitments for the future, may reveal as much or more than the current budget division.

SYSTEMS INTEGRATION

As IT systems start to consist more and more of standard components, so it becomes more urgent to consider who is to integrate the components into complete systems. In the long run, it is likely to be the corporate IT departments themselves who will perform this task. However, since open systems are still a new development, most IT departments will as yet be unused to the process. Small IT departments may find that the task is beyond their resources and automatically seek an outside agency to perform systems integration.

If systems integration is not to be performed internally, either in the short term or as a matter of policy, then preferred suppliers of this service must be chosen. An obvious source is one of the many systems houses that have traditionally provided turnkey systems for proprietary environments. Although systems houses can be expected to have the general skills required, it is important to ascertain whether they have experience with open systems, and more specifically, which kinds of open systems. Most are not large enough to carry expertise in all areas, and may specialise in, for instance, UNIX systems or local-area networking only. Enquiring about actual projects completed successfully, as potential references, is a good way to separate hard experience from claims of expertise.

However, there are other potential sources of systems integration. The time has long gone when the IT industry could be divided easily into suppliers of hardware, software and services. Most of what have traditionally been regarded as hardware suppliers, for instance, now derive a large part of their revenues (sometimes as much as half) from the supply of software and services. Suppliers of open systems in particular have tended to foresee that users will need help in creating working systems, and some are specifically allocating resources to integration services.

An advantage of the traditional hardware vendors is that they typically already have the critical size necessary to carry the range of skills needed for complete systems integration. They are much less likely to be narrowly specialised than systems houses. A disadvantage is that they may be unenthusiastic about the prospect, if offered, of integrating components that are entirely sourced elsewhere. The most obvious case for using them as a systems integrator arises when they are also supplying some of the system components.

As with systems houses, it will be important to probe their actual experience. In both cases the quality and extent of support on offer will be as important as evidence of integration skills. Support should ideally extend to training, education and documentation as well as to the more obvious areas of maintenance and trouble-shooting (which, incidentally, should include a "hot-line"). Training should cover not just the specifics of particular systems but also education in concepts and in aspects of systems integration; if bringing systems integration in-house is a longer-term goal, your current integrator should be able to bring in-house staff up to speed.

FOCUS ON BUSINESS SOLUTIONS

It is important always to bear in mind that the ultimate purpose of any IT system is to provide a business service, cost-effectively. That needs stating because in the current state of the art there are some situations that open systems cannot yet cope with adequately. For projects in which fairly sophisticated wide-area networking is involved, for instance, an OSI solution may prove unacceptably expensive or not even be available at all.

Obviously, a commitment to open systems cannot be allowed to override normal business considerations of cost-effectiveness. If there appears currently to be no open-systems solution to the business system you require, or only a very inelegant or costly one, it is better to admit rather than fight the fact, and go for a proprietary solution.

In such cases, there are still two factors to consider. Firstly, make sure you have taken account of full life-cycle costs in reaching your conclusion. In the current state of the art, open systems are sometimes marginally less cost-effective in the short-term but more cost-effective over time. Secondly, take interoperability between open and proprietary systems into account when making your choice of proprietary system. If your company is committed to moving to open systems, then a new proprietary system will almost certainly have to coexist effectively with open systems at some time, even if not immediately.

The true case for open systems is a practical one, not a theoretical one. Although they already offer many advantages, they are still in the early stages of development. The really important imperative is to avoid, wherever possible, building up general investment in proprietary environments. Short-term proprietary solutions to specific problems, if not desirable, should not be ruled out if they clearly provide the best answer. Avoid open-systems dogma.

HARDWARE CONSIDERATIONS

The major change in hardware that affects open systems is the move to use commodity chip sets as a basis for processor design. Motorola, Intel, MIPS and Sun produce the most widely used chip sets. The use of these chip sets has considerable bearing on the compatibility of processors, so it is worth enquiring whether they are used in a supplier's processors. Conversely, the use of custom-built chips will tend to lock you into the particular supplier's machines.

Another important hardware consideration is the bus architecture. There are two general standards today: one is IBM's Micro Channel Architecture (MCA); the other is the Extended Industry Standard Architecture (EISA), which is a development of the PC AT bus structure and was promoted initially by Compaq. The VMEbus is also widely used, and the Futurebus+ (a development of the VMEbus) is widely tipped as a future standard.

A final, general consideration with any supplier's range of machines is to ask about the range of power offered within the one architecture. Most systems of any importance require a range of different CPUs, most obviously a central CPU and PCs, but often with some intermediate CPUs networked in between. Also, if one has a reasonably wide range of CPU power available within the one architecture, with reasonably small increments in power between machines, this allows good flexibility when future upgrade requirements are uncertain (as they usually are).

SOFTWARE CONSIDERATIONS

UNIX is inevitably the focus of software attention. All suppliers will owe allegiance to either UNIX International or the Open Software Foundation; a few are allied to both.

If you already have UNIX systems of one flavour or another, you should enquire as to the availability of any supplier's software in your flavour. If you don't, you should enquire about any extensions the supplier has made to the original UNIX to counter its inadequacies. These are most notably to do with security, handling commercial files and allowing multiprocessors (symmetric multiprocessing).

As longer-term considerations, you should ask about conformity to X/Open and POSIX standards. A lot has been written about battles over the various flavours of UNIX, but there can be little doubt that the operating system will effectively be standardised before long. "Effectively" means here that any differences will be largely cosmetic, to save the face of one camp or the other. Route maps to the holy grail of one true standard, and dates of availability for particular milestones along the way, are other matters you can question.

Finally on software, it is useful to ask about binary compatibility. A number of standard application binary interfaces (ABIs) have been created for the most widely used commodity chip sets to allow the provision of "shrink-wrapped" software. This is application software that can be loaded and used directly without the need for prior compilation; it will run under UNIX on any machine that uses the same commodity chip set. It is useful to know which software suppliers are lined up behind each ABI, as an indication of how much shrink-wrapped software is (and will be) available on systems using that ABI.

NETWORK CONSIDERATIONS

As has been suggested earlier, whilst OSI is intended (and likely) to become the eventual answer to inter-system networking, it still has a long way to go for many purposes. The X.25, X.400 and X.500 protocols are widely implemented, and are useful for many purposes, so it is worth enquiring whether suppliers have implementations of them.

If OSI won't do the job for you now, or only at unacceptable expense, all is not lost. The communications services provided with most UNIX systems conform to the TCP/IP protocols. Although TCP/IP is not a framework for the future, it is a set of standards that is widely implemented now and is non-proprietary. Ask suppliers whether they provide implementations.

The de facto standard for most large area networks is SNA. Proprietary as it is, it is too important to ignore. Any supplier dedicated to open systems should acknowledge its significance by providing products with good compatibility with it.

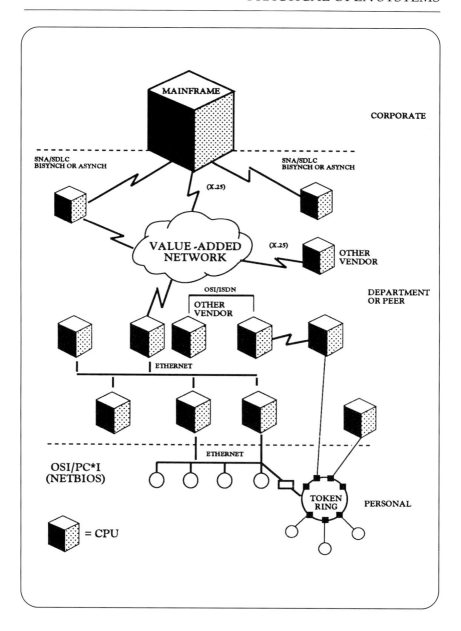

Figure 13.1   Mainframe Environment Topology Chart

For local area networks, there are both the network itself and the network-operating systems to be considered. Three major standards share the LAN market: Ethernet, Token Ring and Starlan. It could be useful to have all three available to you (Figure 13.1). For

LAN operating systems, the prime contenders are NetWare and LAN Manager; look for both.

SUMMARY

The argument for open systems is not a theoretical one; it is a practical answer for today. However, until standards for all aspects of IT have been defined by ISO and implemented by most suppliers, the practical case will involve practical compromises. Already the work of ISO and other standards organisations has forced owners of proprietary environments to make them more open and capable of interoperating with truly open systems. Many existing standards created by alliances of suppliers are to that extent only half-open, but half-way to heaven is better than nowhere at all.

The practical case for open systems is practical precisely because it acknowledges that progress must proceed a step at a time, each step providing more openness than the one before. That is the attitude you should be looking for from suppliers, and you should be able to find it in their products and services. Do not accept impracticability as an excuse for an inadequate product range; it is likely to be simply an excuse for persistence with proprietary solutions.

Appendix 1
Glossary

This glossary is designed primarily as a reference for recall, after the main part of the book has been read. Most of the terms included are explained (often at greater length) where they are used in the main body of the text. Where explanations differ slightly between the main text and the glossary, this is because it is appropriate to give a slightly different slant on a term.

Acronyms are a common handicap to those who do not know what they mean, so acronyms have been given priority over the corresponding full version of the term. If there is a term for which you need an explanation and you cannot find it in the glossary, try forming the initial letters into an acronym and look for that. The explanations given in the glossary are just that—not formal definitions.

The glossary should include all terms used that may need explanation, and a number of others not used in the text have been added. The intention of this book is to provide a broad introduction, focused on directions rather than details, and so many readers may want to explore aspects of the subject in more detail. The additions to the glossary should help in this second-level exploration of the subject, and should enhance the objective of this book to be a first-level source of explanation and reference.

Relatively few additions have been made, necessarily; there are already other glossaries—of IBM systems terminology, for instance—that are longer than this entire book. However, the few that have been added should prove generally relevant.

As regards the index at the end of this book, an effort has been made to avoid referring the reader to the same information as is contained in the glossary, or to trivial occurrences of the word or term. Any page reference shown should add information. Where an item has a major reference point among more minor ones, the major reference point is highlighted.

ABI

Application binary interface: a standard interface to a processor chip set at the executable-code level. ABIs have been, or are being, developed for most of the commodity chip sets.

AD/Cycle

IBM's architecture for the software development environment.

AIA

Applications Integrated Architecture: Digital's architecture for applications—broadly equivalent to IBM's SAA.

AIX

IBM's version of UNIX.

ANSI

The American National Standards Institute: the US equivalent to the BSI—particularly active in language standardisation.

API

Application programming interface: a standard interface between an application program and some set of services, such as those provided by an operating system, a communications system, etc.

Architecture

A broad term that denotes a description of some significant part of a computer system or of an aspect of computing (eg operations, development). An architecture is similar to a standard in that its scope may be small or large, and in that it is an abstraction that can be implemented in more than one way, be it hardware or software. Purists will insist that an architecture should be at a consistent level of abstraction and take no account of inferior levels. In practice the term is used more generally.

BCS
Binary Compatible Standard: the name given to the standard, including an ABI, that allows shrink-wrapped software for an operating system and chip set combination.

Benchmark
This term has the same meaning in computing, if not the same significance, as in its more general use; it is a kind of standard for comparing different systems. In practice, benchmarks do not work well in IT, because of the difficulty in accounting for differences between systems and how applications to run on them are configured. Various "standard" benchmarks have been proposed, notably for comparing on-line transaction processing systems (TP1 and TP2). They are good for providing broad delineations, but can otherwise generally be dismissed as a marketing game for fun (in the current state of the art).

BSD
Berkeley Software Distribution, in conjunction with UNIX, is an early development of UNIX at the University of California at Berkeley that gained wide usage.

BSI
British Standards Institution: the UK national standards-setting body.

Bus
A structure that is used for connecting processors and peripherals, either within a system or, as in this book, in a LAN.

C
A language with exceptional portability, used very widely to program software that is intended to be ported to many different *platforms* (qv). It is essentially a language for systems programmers, and is not one that is appropriate for users to write application programs in.

C++   A variant of the C language that is designed for programming object-oriented systems.

CAD/CAM   Computer-Aided Design/Computer-Aided Manufacturing: an important application that is generally associated with workstations and UNIX, and that may be in the van of progress in object orientation.

CCITT   Consultative Committee for International Telephony and Telegraphy: a UN sub-agency of the International Telecommunications Union; it is the primary formal international agency for telecommunications standards.

CEN   Comité Européen de Normalisation (European Committee for Standardisation): a European Community voice providing an intermediate level of standardisation between national and international standards.

CENELEC   Comité Européen de Normalisation de l'Electrotechnique (European Committee for Electrotechnical Standardisation): a specialised branch of CEN, corresponding at the European level to the IEC.

CEPT   Conférence Européenne des Administrations des Postes et des Télécommunications (European Conference for the Administration of Post and Telecommunications): a European equivalent to the CCITT.

Circuit switching   A means of connecting any two points on a network whereby a circuit between the two points is reserved for the entire transaction. The circuit is first established, the transaction carried out, and then the circuit is disconnected (cf packet switching; see also virtual circuit switching).

CISC
Complex Instruction Set Computer: one with a relatively large instruction set, typically of 300+ instructions, including some very complex operations. Until recently, most computers were designed as CISC machines (cf *RISC*).

Commodity chip sets
Chip sets that have gained such general usage and have such a relatively low price that they can be regarded as commodities.

Compatibility
The property that enables two different systems to be connected and work together for specific practical purposes.

Conformance testing
The testing of devices claimed to conform to certain standards to establish whether they actually do so.

COS
Corporation for Open Systems: an association of users and suppliers that promotes open systems and specifically provides test scripts for OSI conformance testing.

CUE
Common user environment: an environment for applications that frees them from specific dependencies on other software or hardware devices by placing APIs between them and such other entities.

DECNET
Digital's architecture for networks.

De facto (standards)
Standards that have arisen through wide general usage rather than through any conscious standards-establishment process.

DISC
A group within the British Standards Institution that deals specifically with IT standards.

DTI
Department of Trade and Industry: a UK

government department (equivalent to the US Department of Commerce) which has adopted a policy of promoting open systems.

ECMA   European Computer Manufacturers' Association: a consortium of European computer vendors (though some American vendors have joined more recently). It provides input to various formal standards bodies.

EDI   Electronic document interchange: the exchange of documents relating to commercial transactions (eg orders, invoices, etc) by electronic means.

EDIFACT   A proposed standard for EDI that is being developed by ISO.

EISA   Extended Industry Standard Architecture: the name applied to a group of PC suppliers seeking to perpetuate and extend in a standard form the original bus architecture of the IBM PC; the name is also applied to the standard itself. The incentive for this standard is so that users wishing to do so can avoid the switch to the Micro Channel Architecture that IBM has adopted for its second-generation PCs, the PS/2s (cf *MCA*).

Ethernet   A structure for local area networks, based on a bus and originating in work carried out by Xerox; the associated protocols have been subjected to standardisation as IEEE 802.3.

EurOSInet   A consortium of European vendors, the purpose of which is to demonstrate and promote the practicality of OSI networking.

FDDI	Fibre Distributed Data Interface: an ANSI standard for transmissions over fibre-optic cable which is growing fast in importance.
FTAM	File Transfer, Access and Management: an ISO standard (ISO 8571) for the transfer (and access and management) of files across an OSI network.
FTP	The TCP/IP protocol for file transfer.
Functional standards	A subset of a body of standards that is recommended for general implementation. Essentially, functional standards are designed to isolate standards that are adequate for most general cases from the more esoteric ones, to reduce the cost of implementation and minimise interconnection difficulties.
Gateway	A general term for a mechanism (hardware and/or software) that allows access between two networks working to different protocols.
GOSIP	Government OSI Profile: a set of OSI functional standards defined by a government agency.
GUI	Graphical user interface: involving the use of graphics as the primary means of communication between users and computer systems. GUIs are becoming subject to standardisation.
Icon	A graphical image on a computer screen used to denote an object (typically a file or a process) that the user can interact with.
IEC	International Electrotechnical Committee: the UN agency concerned with electrotechnical standards.

IEE   Institute of Electrical Engineers: the UK professional body for electrical engineers—the counterpart to the IEEE in the US.

IEEE   Institute of Electrical and Electronic Engineers: the US equivalent of the IEE in the UK, with a similar role in establishing standards.

Interoperability   The ability of systems of different architectures to pass data and commands to one another to a useful extent, and to interpret the information passed correctly.

IRDS   Information Resource Dictionary System: the ISO proposed standard for an information repository and the eventual open-systems version of, for instance, Repository Manager/MVS.

ISDN   Integrated Services Digital Network: an evolving CCITT standard for the integration of voice, data and images over the same circuits in a digital network.

IT   Information technology: a term used predominantly in the UK—broadly equivalent to IS (information services) and MIS (management information systems) as used in other countries.

ITSU   Information Technology Standards Unit: the department within the DTI charged specifically with the promotion of open-systems standards.

LAN   Local area network: a network used typically to link small computers (such as PCs) and associated peripherals that are located reasonably close to one another, usually in the same building.

LAN Manager   A LAN operating system developed by

	Microsoft for token-ring networks that has achieved considerable importance.
Life-cycle	A term used frequently in connection with software development and also (in this book) with costing; it denotes a consideration of the totality of a process, or the entire consequences of a decision, from the very outset.
LU6.2	The IBM standard, within SNA, for performing basic peer-to-peer communications.
MAP	Manufacturing Automation Protocols: a set of standards developed by General Motors for use in production automation.
MCA	Micro Channel Architecture: the bus structure designed by IBM for its second-generation PCs, the PS/2s.
MS-DOS	The PC operating system developed by Microsoft for 16-bit machines that became a de facto industry standard and demonstrated the benefits that open systems and markets can provide.
MVS	The flagship IBM operating system for 370-architecture (large) machines. Its origins, some of which are unfortunately still discernible, go all the way back to OS/360 in the mid-1960s. It has proved to have incredible longevity and has achieved close to a worldwide monopoly of large mainframe environments. Its richness in function, and the wide third-party market it has spawned, compensate for its ungainliness and the historical baggage it has to carry.
NAS	Network Application Support: a Digital architecture for distributed applications.

NCC	National Computing Centre: a UK body set up with government support as a centre of computing expertise relating to industry. It provides input to standards bodies.
NetWare	A LAN operating system developed by Novell that has achieved wide usage for Ethernet LANs. It is being brought into conformity with OSI standards.
New Wave	A graphical user interface developed by Hewlett-Packard.
NFS	A standard for file transfer between UNIX systems developed by Sun.
Object-oriented system	A system that deals primarily with objects rather than data, images, text, etc, explicitly.
OLTP	On-line transaction processing: a generic term for applications that involve a (usually large) number of (normally local) terminals entering a (similarly large) number of transactions that have to be processed very speedily. Banking cash terminals and order entry are fair examples. The number of applications of this type is on the increase, as customer service is becoming perceived as more important. Partly for this reason, OLTP is frequently mentioned in conjunction with *benchmarks* (qv).
Open Look	A graphical user interface developed by AT&T.
Open systems	As used in this book, systems that do not conform to an architecture that is significantly controlled by a single vendor with a relatively small market base and a sparse third-party market. Purists might insist that only systems that conform

	totally to formal international standards can be described as open.
OS/2	The operating system designed by IBM for its PS/2 PCs. It is competing for market share with UNIX.
OSF	Open Software Foundation: an alliance of suppliers to create standards (and implementations of them) for the UNIX operating system. It does not include AT&T.
OSF/Motif	A graphical user interface designed by OSF which is gaining support within UI.
OSI	Open Systems Interconnection: the evolving body of standards that is being developed by ISO for the interconnection of different computer systems within a network.
OSITOP	A user group that provides a channel for user recommendations to the OSI standardisation committee.
Packet switching	A method of passing information between any two points in a network in units (packets). The information to be passed is disassembled into packets on entry into the network, and packets then proceed individually by any available route to their destination. Before leaving the network, the packets are reassembled into their original form.
PC-DOS	The IBM operating system for its first PCs—a variant of MS-DOS.
PCTE	Portable Common Tools Environment: part of the emerging ISO standard environment for software development.
Platform	A general term for a range of hardware and/or system software.
Portability	The ability of a program to run on

systems with different architectures.

POSIX   An IEEE standard for interfaces between an operating system and the wider computing environment.

Presentation Manager A graphical user interface developed by IBM.

Profile   A set of functional standards.

Protocol   A convention defined to allow the correct interpretation of information.

Reference model   A map of an area of IT created as a framework for standards formulation.

RISC   Reduced Instruction Set Computer: a relatively new approach to designing computer instruction sets to produce powerful machines more cheaply (cf *CISC*).

RPC   Remote Procedure Call: a mechanism used by most versions of distributed processing systems to allow a program that is running on one processor to cause a procedure to be carried out on another. There is no standard version yet, but one (or more) will undoubtedly be developed as standardisation efforts focus more closely on distributed computing.

RS232C   The most commonly used standard (ANSI) serial interface for physical connection between processors and peripherals.

SAA   Systems Application Architecture: IBM's architecture for applications to run on its major platforms.

Scalability   The property of ranges of machines that allows upgrades in power to be made in very small increments.

SNA	Systems Network Architecture: the wide-area network architecture designed by IBM for networking its computer systems. It is the most important network architecture today.
SQL	A database query language developed originally by IBM and now subjected to international standardisation effort. It is proposed as a standard interface between applications programs and database systems. The first attempt at standardisation has met with considerable criticism because it lacks certain necessary features, and furthermore standardisation will be needed. Additions to allow for object orientation are one area of concern.
Starlan	A variant of the Ethernet LAN architecture that uses a star rather than a bus structure.
SVID	System V Interface Definition: the basis of most current versions of UNIX, and an important part of the basis for the standardisation of UNIX.
TCP/IP	Transmission Control Protocol/Internet Protocol: two sets of complementary protocols developed under the auspices of the US Department of Defense to Standardise networking between their systems. Because they were defined early on, have to be provided by all systems tendered to the US DoD and are not "owned" by any computer vendor, these protocols have gained wide usage, particularly in conjunction with UNIX systems.
Token Ring	A LAN structure based on token-passing round a ring (or, more accurately, along a queue) of devices; it has been subjected to standardisation as IEEE 802.5.

TOP   Technical and Office Protocols: a set of
                           standards for office systems defined ori-
                           ginally by the Boeing company.

UI   UNIX International: an alliance of sup-
                           pliers to create standards (and imple-
                           mentations of them) for the UNIX operat-
                           ing system. It includes AT&T, where
                           UNIX was originally created.

Ultrix   Digital's version of UNIX.

Uniforum   An agency supported by an alliance of
                           major suppliers to provide information
                           and advice on standards, particularly
                           with respect to UNIX.

UNIX   The operating system adopted by the
                           open systems movement as the basic
                           operating environment for machines
                           from workstation/large PC size up to
                           high-end mid-range/small mainframe
                           systems. UNIX was originally created by
                           AT&T, and ownership of it has now been
                           placed by AT&T in a subsidiary called
                           UNIX Software Operation.

USO   UNIX Software Operation: the company
                           formed by AT&T to take care of the
                           future development of UNIX.

V24   The CCITT equivalent, more or less, to
                           the ANSI RS232C interface between pro-
                           cessors and peripherals.

Virtual   The term used in computing to denote a
                           logical rather than a physical entity.

Virtual circuit   A technique used in packet-switched
switching   networks to predetermine the routeing of
                           packets through the network. When the
                           first packet passes through, its route is
                           stored for subsequent packets to follow,
                           thus creating a virtual circuit.

VT	Virtual Terminal: a term used for the ISO standards (9040 and 9041) which cope with interfacing different kinds of terminal with open systems.
WAN	Wide area network: a network that covers a wide geographical area and that typically (although not necessarily) uses much lower transmission speeds than a local area network.
X.21	The CCITT standard for communication between user devices in a circuit-switched network.
X.25	The CCITT standard for communication in packet-switched networks.
X.400	The CCITT standard for store-and-forward message handling over networks. It is widely used as a basis for electronic mail in office systems.
X/Open	A consortium of computer vendors charged with creating a multi-vendor common applications environment (CAE) on the basis of the most useful of the formal and de facto standards. This body has been particularly active in UNIX standardisation efforts, and its portability (XPG.3) is widely respected.
X-Windows	A graphical user interface developed at the Massachusetts Institute of Technology (MIT) that has received wide acceptance.
Xenix	An early commercial PC version of UNIX developed by Microsoft and the Santa Cruz Operation which achieved considerable acceptance.

Appendix 2
Questions for open-systems suppliers

BRIEFING NOTES

This checklist of questions is offered to you by Data General as a means of helping you decide which open-systems suppliers you will choose to deal with in the future. Since it is provided by an interested party, it is open to accusations of bias; test it on other suppliers to see if they cry "foul" (and where and why).

The checklist should also help to resolve a common problem at exhibitions or demonstrations: knowing what questions to ask of whom and/or wondering whether you have asked all the relevant questions (particularly those that suppliers will be reluctant to prompt you on).

Whatever other suppliers may say about the checklist, you will certainly learn more by using it than you would otherwise. You will also have more fun. Other suppliers may, in return, suggest questions that you should ask of Data General. If they do, please feel free to ask them.

The checklist has deliberately been made simple, and the questions baldly stated, so that you can use it easily. This book contains the fuller rationale behind the questions.

CHECKLIST OF QUESTIONS

1 If your company operates a preferred suppliers list, are the major criteria for inclusion met?

2 Evidence of commitment to open systems:

— range of involvement across the spectrum;

— involvement in alternative bodies;

— direction of R&D budget.

3 Are systems-integration services offered?

— Do these include solutions consultancy?

— How wide is the supplier's experience?

- MS-DOS systems

- UNIX systems

- connection to mainframe systems

- LANs

- OSI

- TCP/IP

- others.

— How extensive is the support?

- maintenance

- hot-line available

- general education in concepts

- training

- documentation.

4 Proprietary solutions:

— interoperability with open systems generally;

— SNA;

— SAA compliance.

5 Hardware:

   — commodity chip set;

   — bus architecture;

   — power range within a single architecture.

6 Software:

   — UNIX flavour;

   — symmetric multiprocessing;

   — file handling;

   — security;

   — X/Open;

   — POSIX;

   — ABIs.

7 Networks:

   — X.25, X.400, X.500;

   — TCP/IP in product range;

   — SNA compatibility;

   — Ethernet;

   — Token Ring;

   — Starlan.

8 Summary:

   — Is the supplier flexible or wedded to pure dogma?

Appendix 3
Sources of information

There are many sources of help for companies seeking to investigate the feasibility of an open-systems strategy or to implement such a strategy. Many consultants claim to have expertise in this area, but it is difficult to assess the validity of these claims without contacting the consultants individually.

Rather than compile a suspect and probably long list, we have chosen simply to provide the addresses of the major organisations with a significant role in establishing or promoting open systems. Organisations concerned with promoting open systems should be a particularly good source of further information.

Finally, it is always worth seeking further information from any supplier your company is already in contact with that claims an allegiance to open systems. First make sure, though, that you have read and assimilated Chapter 13: *Choosing a supplier*.

ADDRESSES OF STANDARDS ORGANISATIONS

88open
8560 SW Salish Lane
Suite 500
Wilsonville
OR 97070
USA

ANSI
1430 Broadway
New York
NY 10018
USA

BCS
13 Mansfield Street
London
W1M 0BP

BSI
IT Services
Linford Wood
Milton Keynes
MK14 6LE

CCITT
Place des Nations
CH-1211 Geneva 20
Switzerland

COS
1750 Old Meadow Road
Suite 400
McLean
VA 22102
USA

DISC
13 Mansfield Street
London
W17 0BP

DTI
IT Standards Unit
Kingsgate House
66–74 Victoria Street
London
SW1E 6SW

ECMA
Rue du Rhône 114
CH-1211 Geneva
Switzerland

EISA
BCPR Services Inc
1400 Lower Street NW
Washington DC
DC 20005-3502
USA

EurOSInet
c/o Level 7 Ltd
Guildgate House
The Terrace
Wokingham
Berks
RG11 1BP

IEE
2 Savoy Place
London
WC2R 0BL

IEEE
345 East 47th Street
New York
NY 10017-2394
USA

NCC
Oxford Road
Manchester
M1 7ED

NIST
Washington DC
DC 20402
USA

OMG
Framingham Corporate Center
492 Old Connecticut Path
Framingham
MA 01701
USA

OSF
11 Cambridge Center
Cambridge
MA 02142
USA

OSITOP

21 Avenue de Messina
75008 Paris
France

OSNMF

40 Morristown Road
Bernardsville
NJ 07924
USA

Uniforum

Gate House
1/3 St Johns Square
London
EC1M 4DH

Unix International

25 Avenue de Beaulieu
B-1160 Brussels
Belgium

or

Unix International

20 Waterview Blvd
Parsippany
NJ 07054
USA

X/Open

Apex Plaza
Forbury Road
Reading
RG1 1AX

Index